STITCHING IT RIGHT

The Entrepreneurial Journey from A
Car Garage to Harvard

RAJAT SIKKA

STARDOM BOOKS

www.StardomBooks.com

STARDOM BOOKS
A Division of Stardom Publishing
and infoYOGIS Technologies.
105-501 Silverside Road
Wilmington, DE 19809

FIRST EDITION APRIL 2022

STARDOM BOOKS

A Division of Stardom Alliance
105-501 Silverside Road Wilmington, DE 19809,
USA

www.stardombooks.com

Stardom Books, United States
Stardom Books, India

STITCHING IT RIGHT
The Entrepreneurial Journey from A Car Garage to
Harvard

Rajat Sikka

p. 140
cm. 13.97 X 21.59

Category:
BUS025000 Business & Economics:
Entrepreneurship
SEL027000 Self-Help : Personal Growth – Success

ISBN: 978-1-957456-04-1

DEDICATION

This book is dedicated to the CEO of our company, Shirdi Sai Baba without whose blessings this journey would not have started and who has guided and mentored us through all the hard times. It is also dedicated to my father, Late R.P.Sikka who guided and protected us in spirit

For Vandana, whose passion was the heart and soul of Saivana and the forever COO of the company.

For Ahvana, my Bollywood baby who will one day surely dominate the global silver screen.

For Uvanka, my rebel baby, who will one day shine through the clouds and make humanity proud of her.

CONTENTS

ACKNOWLEDGMENTS

I would like to acknowledge the hard-working people of Saivana who have been the real backbone of the company

I also would like to acknowledge our suppliers and last but not least, a big shout-out, to our buyers who have given us the privilege of being part of their own growth journeys.

A special shout-out goes to Sanjay Khanna, Mohit Soni, and Sudhir Oberoi who helped at very key moments when Saivana really needed its friends.

1
THE BACKBENCHER'S BURGER

0.67. This story begins with the number, 0.67. It might seem arbitrary as it is not even a whole number; I mean, it is not even 1. It is just a tad more than half. However, this number carries great significance in my life. If you were to hazard a guess as to what it stands for, a few of you may even get it right. However, even if you have guessed it right, you might still harbor an inkling of doubt, questioning if this really could be true. "No one is capable of that," you would probably think. People may fail to ascend great heights but no one is capable of having such a great fall, down to rock bottom! Well, here is someone who managed to do exactly that.

This number, which is etched deeply in my memories, is my cumulative Grade Point Average (GPA) in my first semester at Drew University in Madison, New Jersey. How I wish I could say that this was the difference between a perfect GPA and my actual GPA. I wish I could paint a pretty picture of my stellar performance in the first year of my study at Drew. Well, if I did so, I would be lying and you would be left with only an abstract image of my imaginary excellence. The American GPA is measured on a 4-point scale. It is next to impossible for one to get 0.67. I mean, even if you just showed up in class, you were assured of a 1.0 or even 1.5.

Just mere attendance to classes and tests should net you that grade. But here I was, an Indian, sitting in a small New England university with a miserable GPA of 0.67. I had achieved the impossible. But this feat did not warrant the sweet champagne of success; just a mucky feeling of misery remained.

Now, having heard me mention the bare minimum to get a 1 or 1.5 GPA, I am sure that some of you might have a pertinent question. How did this happen? How was I able to score that low? I have a simple answer.

I have always been a backbencher. I was the quintessential poster boy for all the stereotypes that are usually associated with that label. Yes, obviously I will blame this debacle on everything else but myself, but we will come back to that later.

I had come across a quote some time ago. It went like this: *"Backbenchers always think about creating their own company while frontbenchers think only about working in big companies."* I can tell you with relative confidence and personal proof that this quote did manifest itself in my life. I shall broach the topic of my company in the later chapters of this book. However, I started from the backbench. I firmly believe that some of the most successful entrepreneurs have been backbenchers in their lives.

If you were to go by the popular cliches or stereotypes, this may seem impossible to fathom. How can some of the greatest achievers in today's world not be interested in school? We have been brought up with the idea that you need good grades to lead a good life. So, why would they sit at the back of the classroom?

It is a myth that backbenchers are just lazy louts who listen to Pink Floyd and sing aloud the lines 'We Don't Need No Education.' They are much more than such stereotypes. They are the disruptors in an education system that hitherto was only successful in producing students of the same mold. There is a famous Ted Talk by Sir Ken Robinson where he talks of how the modern education system kills creativity. I would highly recommend my readers to listen to his illuminating talk. Let us for a moment indulge in the stereotype of a backbencher.

I have already mentioned that they can be more than just a stereotype; however, I just want to examine the creativity and courage involved in some of their rule-breaking acts. They will find a way to catch a few winks even in the strictest of teachers' classes. Some of them can be quite creative literally: doodling and drawing in the classroom have resulted in the creation of some entertaining pieces of art. Some find the inspiration to pen down a poem. A few others find an opportunity to complete their unfinished homework for the next class. And there are a few who find a way to watch a video or read an extracurricular book. Friends sitting in the backbenches choose to break the monotony of the classes by playing tic-tac-toe surreptitiously. I have even seen some very bold students eating burgers from Nirulas when the teacher's back was turned toward them.

When they turned to face the class after having written something on the blackboard, they would find nary a clue as to the repast enjoyed by the culprits. These guys knew the trick of munching a burger without the slightest noise. I have indulged in many such activities and I really admired some of their daredevilry. How indeed could they resist the gasps of satisfaction and delight when they bit into a juicy burger? I managed to eat my burger in silence, but I had to scrunch my face and close my eyes in delight to compensate for enforced quietness. I always thought some of them could have graced the Louvre for their stoic marble-like visages even as they chewed a delicious burger.

How about we visit the stereotype of the front-bencher? The images that come to mind are obvious. They are the ones who take down copious notes. I even wonder if they transcribe every pause of breath taken by the teacher! One of the iconic examples of a front-bencher has to be the character 'Silencer' from the movie *3 Idiots*. He followed the lines and learned by rote. His infamous speech in the movie showcased this failure of his. How about Amir Khan's character in the same movie? Here was a backbencher who for all intents and purposes ticked off every teacher and sat in at whichever class he could find. That was his creativity and desire to learn.

In my life, I was a backbencher, but not quite in the mold of Amir Khan's character. I did fairly well in my studies. However, I was the guy who would doodle during a particularly boring class. I would also play tic-tac-toe with my neighbor in the classroom. I am not going to lie; I have enjoyed some good burgers in the classroom as well. All these feats required dexterity and creativity. Well, I was also caught a few times. One cannot be successful all the time. Those occasions saw me and my friends visit the Principal's office. We were caned for our troubles. However, we saw the cane marks on our palms as scars of honor!

However, when you are caught more than once, you are identified as a repeat offender. This means you become the object of conspicuous scrutiny by your teachers. This only adds to the challenge. We had to learn to be more creative and audacious. We looked at it as a game or a war that we had to win. I can tell you with some relative pride that we got away more times than we were caught.

In hindsight, I can say with confidence that those feats in the backbenches laid the foundations of my entrepreneurial life. Today, when I look back, I realize that most of those students who sat in the front rows of my class ended up in service jobs, banks, etc., while the guys in the back became successful businessmen. You could say it mirrored the characters in 3 Idiots almost perfectly. There is another wonderful saying about backbenchers that I have come across: *"Backbenchers are the ones who sleep during the lectures but they dream with their eyes open."*

There is a reason I have brought up the idea of dreams. But for that let us go back to the number with which I started this chapter, 0.67. My GPA was 0.67. I was embarrassed. However, misery always loves company. I received a letter in the mail from the Dean's office. I knew that this would not be good news. It was not. I was informed that my scholarship was being withdrawn. There is a superstitious belief that misfortune comes in threes. It could be a myth, but unfortunately, it turned true in my case. I received another letter. This letter informed me that I was being rusticated.

However, owing to my never-say-die attitude cultivated in my life as a backbencher, I was not that bothered. Even in the face of what seemed like an apocalypse, I was not devastated. I may have also been the first Indian student to have lost his whole scholarship in the first semester. Even this fact did not bother me. I must clarify that I was not nonchalant. I was scared of what my present and my future held. But I was not devastated, probably because I knew I had it coming.

Now, the preceding statement might pique your curiosity. How did I know I had it coming? Details about my first semester at Drew in America would clarify this doubt. I think I possibly gave a clue earlier in this chapter. Mere attendance would allow you to score a GPA of 1 or 1.5. I was not in New Jersey during my first semester. I was much further down south, on the beaches of Florida and the Bahamas. There was always a new party going on there. Americans follow the concept of spring break. After I landed in America, I took my entire first semester as a spring break. If I was not on the beaches, I would have been at the roulette and blackjack tables in the casinos of Las Vegas and Atlantic City. When I felt particularly adventurous, I also tried my hand at poker. My idea was to strike it rich and become known as the next richest Indian on the North American subcontinent.

Well, you do not need a fortune teller to tell you that this was not a good idea. I had wasted away my money. Then I lost my scholarship, and as the cherry on the top, I was even thrown out of my university. My poor parents thought that I had succumbed to drugs because nothing else could explain this dismal performance. I mean there was no other plausible explanation they could think of other than "my Munda is now into drugs".

It was not a flattering picture and it was especially aggravating to me that after had I spent so much time talking about how the backbencher is more than the stereotype, I eventually became one myself. I went from a well-functioning backbencher in the classroom to a ghostly presence in one. I had become persona non grata in an alien country. There seemed to be no way to bounce back.

I had lost all my money. My girlfriends at Drew also disappeared (oh, some of these Bollywood movies have so many clichés). I felt the world spinning out of control. I had no idea what to do and I seemed lost. Slap! A resounding thud on my cheeks woke me up and showed me the direction forward. I was at the receiving end of a slap from my father. It was as if my vision had cleared. I recognized that my father had flown in all the way from India to wake me up. I have no complaints as that slap was well-deserved. I was now determined to make amends. I had to ensure that I did not become the big failure that my circumstances seemed to point to at that moment in my life. I wanted to be more than that and do better. So, I decided to visit the Dean and ask for another opportunity.

I still remember the day I visited the Dean's office as if it was yesterday. It was snowing very heavily that day (New Jersey, I tell you). And the situation was quite corny: I was being frozen out of my university and I was looking for some thawing from the Dean. I went into her office and begged her for another chance. I told her that in High School, I had been in the top 20 percent of my class; I had been the debating club President, Chairman of the Model United Nations, and the Editor-in-Chief of my school newspaper. These facts were not news to her.

I knew she was aware of them because it was all mentioned in my college application. I asked her to give me one last chance. I upped the stakes by adding that if by the end of the next semester, I did not get a GPA of 3.75 and above, I would leave the college voluntarily. She was very skeptical upon hearing my request. She explained that she had felt particularly blindsided by me. She had personally cleared my admission into the college and had been shocked when she saw my results. She had put her faith in me and I had taken a sledgehammer to her expectations and crushed it into bits. She did not know if she could trust me. I did not have any explanations or excuses to give. What could I say in my defense? I could not say that I lost my compass upon landing in America. I could not tell her that the neon and psychedelic lights had dazzled my eyes and blinded me from going down the right path.

I had lost sight of what I was supposed to achieve in my life. I looked her in the eye and appealed to the American system of justice and fair trial. I spoke about the American Dream. Even a condemned man was given one last chance to find redemption and atone for his mistakes. We talked for an hour. It seemed longer to me as my fate was hanging in the balance. I convinced her to take a chance on me. The Dean was finally convinced; however, she had a few conditions from her side. The first one was that I had to maintain a GPA of 3.75 and above. The second condition was that I had to do 200 hours of community service. The final condition was that I had to take up a campus job to support myself. If I think about it today, I think the final condition was part of a deal struck between my dad and her. I think it was his way of ensuring that I remained on campus. But we will never know what really happened.

The next four years of my life were just about studies. I am not saying that I turned over a new leaf and became a completely new person overnight. I was never stuck to my books. I did party (come on, once a party animal, always a party animal), but in moderation. I was forced to take a job as a campus security guard. Can you imagine, me, a 5-foot-6-inch Indian, patrolling the campus trying to portray myself as Clint Eastwood or, as some old-timers might recollect, TJ Hooker (no sly grins please)?

However, this job and the hours spent in community service instilled humility within me. It taught me the importance of money and hard work. There is no substitute for hard work and there are no shortcuts in life. The 0.67 GPA was the reality check I needed in my life. The best backbenchers transcend the stereotypes. They are not satisfied with their typecast image. In my case, I had pushed the boundaries to a point where I was no longer in control. I had learned one valuable lesson after the debacle of my first semester: Do not let things get out of control because then you will always be at the mercy of others.

Life in America changed me in a lot of ways. America is indeed one of the world's greatest countries and my college taught me how to be respectful toward all religions.

It taught me that everyone had equal rights. More importantly, it also taught me that hard work will eventually be rewarded. The American Dream is not just advertising bluster. I am a living example of it. America has always rewarded hard work and out-of-the-box thinking. The main reason for this is the freedom afforded by US colleges. They give you the space to experiment with new ideas and to pursue what you feel is best for you. I went to Drew to pursue a bachelor's degree in Economics. When I graduated from college, I did it with a double major in Economics and Political Science. I loved Political Science and, in fact, I went on to become the first Indian to become the President of Drew College Republicans.

I became the President at a time when I had no idea what it meant to be a Democrat or a Republican. They made me the President because they wanted to show their sense of diversity. It was hilarious. The only Indian on campus was made the President. I learned that holding a responsible position in that prestigious organization meant that I also had to do all the heavy lifting. However, I built a lot of relationships and camaraderie when I served in that post. I even remember campaigning for a local New Jersey senatorial race. I made flyers and distributed them in the freezing sleet as we went canvassing. It was for a New Jersey native by the name of Joe Bubba (yeah, that sounds a very 'New Jersey' type of name). As the President of the Drew College Republicans, I also canvassed the streets of New Jersey and answered phones to garner votes for Mr. Bubba.

I can say with great pride that none of my efforts were wasted. A wonder of wonders, the Republican candidate actually won! We were even invited to a celebration party as a reward for our efforts. It was one of the best parties that I had ever attended as a college student (perhaps, I should stop referring to the endless parties)! However, picture this scene: I walked into the party with my shoulder-length flowing hair. I also had a good beard game going on at that point and I was wearing a kurta. I immediately attracted attention as I looked like a mystical guru from India. Perhaps, there is an alternative career there to be pursued.

Eventually, I had to graduate. So, I had made sure that when the graduation day rolled around, I was indeed going to graduate from Drew University, Madison, NJ without any more hiccups. I had kind of kept my promise to my Dean of attaining a cumulative 3.75 GPA (mathematically it was not possible after the 0.67 in the first semester), but in my last semester, I made it to the Dean's List with a superlative 3.97 GPA. The only subject where I choked was (okay, this is embarrassing) Religions of India (the professor gave me an A instead of an A+). I called all my friends for my graduation and they graciously accepted my invitation.

On the eve of graduation, I hosted one of the biggest parties on campus. However, because of the distance, my parents could not come to my party...I meant graduation. I woke up with a start the next morning and was taken aback when I looked at the time. Holy smokes! The biggest day of my life, and I had overslept! I looked across the room and saw my friends still snoring away. Some of them had not even bothered to look for a bed or a cushion and had just slept on the floor.

I quickly freshened up and dashed to the ceremony. I was wearing my black graduation gown and hat and rushed to the ground. I had one thing going for me and that was my last name, Sikka. Now, you may wonder why I say this. It is not a name that carries power like a Rothschild or Tata. Sikka had one commonality with those two famous names.

In America, the names are called out in alphabetical order during the graduation ceremony, and Sikka comes down in the list alphabetically. I was thankful for my surname being Sikka as the ceremony had only progressed till the Gs when I reached my seat. Once I was seated, a bottle of champagne was passed to me. Most of my fellow soon-to-be graduates were carrying bottles of champagne under their robes.

So, at 9 am, hungover and sweating from my headlong rush to the ceremony, I had a full swig of champagne to celebrate. It was time to celebrate because there had been a time when I thought I would never see this day.

I got my degree and went back to my dorm to further celebrate with my friends who, again I must emphasize, had come down for my graduation but were still sleeping. I tell you what a great friendship!

What next after America? I was not ready for my next adventure. I wanted to work but my father had other ideas. He wanted me to get an MBA degree. I thought California would be great (no, the idea of awesome beaches and long drives in a convertible did not spring even once to my mind) but Dad had other ideas. He had already secured admission for me in a small college in Switzerland called Business School Lausanne (BSL). In addition, his best friend Mr. Karam Chand lived in nearby Geneva, and he was made my local guardian. My father attributed all my misdeeds in America to my interest in only making girlfriends (I swear on vodka, that was not the case, but then again, I never drank vodka); so, he decided to take them out of the equation.

How? It was a simple but brilliant strategy: I would be given just about enough money for my living expenses and nothing else. If there was no money, one could not woo a lady by taking her out on a nice date. Now he took the help of the one institution that even the Gods shuddered at when they had to deal with them: the Swiss Banks. An account was opened in a Swiss bank in my name and instructions were given to adhere. The account would release an allowance only on the 1st and 15th of every month and it would come up to 1000 Swiss Francs. I must tell you that I saw what abject poverty was like in affluent Switzerland. At that time, and even now, the famous Big Mac burgers cost the maximum in Switzerland. A 1000 Francs for 15 days was just not enough.

I was not even allowed any grace days. Suppose Switzerland had holidays from, say, the 12th to the 16th of a particular month, it was not possible for me to get my money on the 11th. I had to go to Geneva on the 15th or after the 15th but NEVER before that date. I must say I have never liked Swiss banks ever since. There were times when I had to borrow money from my friends for the train ride to Geneva from Lausanne.

On a few occasions, I would reach there and find out that the bank was closed due to some national holiday or the other (remember, Google aunty was not around those days to keep me updated) and then I had to spend the days and nights with my local guardian as I waited for the banks to open. So, it was a very tough period. I also had picked up the habit of smoking and I found that it was an expensive habit to maintain.

Life was tough but one good result came out of the experience. Since I did not have money to splurge on or take even a girl out for a date (heaven forbid if she asked to have a glass of wine), I focused on my studies and I graduated in the top 2 percent of the class. BSL was a small school, often overshadowed by its huge contemporary IMEDE. When I used to tell people I studied in Lausanne, they would always assume it had to be IMEDE (which is the equivalent of Harvard in Europe) and I must confess, there were times I did not contradict them. Hey, I am a Punjabi after all, and showing off is in my DNA. BSL was a small college and I soon realized that only students from affluent families studied there. The daughter of the President of Kyrgyzstan (a country I had never heard of until then) was a student at BSL as was the nephew (or cousin, I was never sure) of Muhammad Gaddafi of Libya. All of these guys used to come for their classes in their swanky cars, whereas there I was, a student who had to take the Metro to the college every day (I know readers, you must be having tears in your eyes).

The only thing I hated in the MBA course was the Finance classes. I just hated numbers and I had no love for concepts like NAV, Acid Test ratio, etc. In hindsight, I definitely wish I had done things differently and paid more attention to the Finance classes. But I excelled in my Marketing classes, topping each one of them easily. I had a flair for marketing and by the time I graduated from BSL, I knew marketing was where I was going to be. Unfortunately, just before I graduated from BSL, a phone call changed my life. I received a call at 3 am one day informing me that my father had passed away. That was one of the most devastating blows I have received in my life.

I wish he could have seen me graduating *magna cum laude* and making it to the Dean's list. To date, I have never gotten over that 3 am call from Indonesia and even now I get startled and alarmed if a phone rings in the middle of the night. It was a life-changing event and it totally shattered me. My father was a visionary of his times. An engineer by profession, he had a heart of gold and did not indulge in the normal Punjabi gossip and politics. He left that to my mother. He was a role model in my life and his friendship with Karam Chand uncle taught me the essence of a good friendship. I always found it amusing that they used to do their "accounts" over a bottle of wine. The exercise was usually completed in 10 minutes and my mother always suspected that my father was being short-changed by my uncle (but it was never the case).

To date, whenever people talk about my father, they only have great things to say. He was an avid bridge player and when I was young, he always encouraged me to take part in extracurricular activities such as tennis, cricket, debating, elocution, drama, etc. Yes, like any parent, he got really alarmed after my 0.67 GPA, but on the whole, I think he knew I would do alright in life. I must credit him for my liberal thinking today and my overall attitude to life. But on that fateful day, I was a bit lost. He was gone and it was time for me to grow up.

I had no idea of the real world as my parents had sheltered me throughout my life. I had only visited India during my holidays and I had no idea how things moved there. Once I graduated from BSL, I took a lonely flight back to India. I had no father to pat me on the back and congratulate me on a job well done. I had to return to a life where I did not have my father with me anymore. I remember crying throughout the flight as the last time I had met him was in Lausanne. He had come to see the Dean of the College and inquire about my progress. Soon after my return, I went on to accept a 9-to-5 job, joining the ranks of what society deemed as civilized employment. I had gone from being a backbencher to a regular office goer. I had taken the safe route, same as what most of the much-vaunted frontbenchers had done.

But I soon realized, my future did not lie on that path. I would eventually hew my path forward by cutting threads in the middle of Okhla, New Delhi. I would tread the illustrious path of backbenchers who started their own companies and became a success. This is my journey as an entrepreneur with *Saivana*.

"Twenty years from now you will be more disappointed by the things that you didn't do than by the ones you did do. So throw off the bowlines. Sail away from the safe harbor. Catch the trade winds in your sails. Explore. Dream. Discover."

- Mark Twain

2
THE FRENCH ONION SOUP

"The garage is the space for the hacker, the tinkerer, the maker. The garage is not defined by a single field or industry; instead, it is defined by the eclectic interests of its inhabitants. It is a space where intellectual networks converge." — Steven Johnson, How We Got to Now: Six Innovations That Made the Modern World

What do Amazon, Microsoft, Disney, Apple, Google, Harley Davidson, Hewlett-Packard, Mattel, Del, and Nike have in common? The obvious answer would be they are all leading business giants from the United States of America. They can be seen as the perfect representation of the American Dream.

But if you dig a little deeper, you will find that Jeff Bezos started his enterprise as an online bookstore out of his home garage in 1994. Although it took him a year to sell his first book, Amazon is a juggernaut in e-commerce today. Paul Allen and Bill Gates wrote codes to program their first operating system from a small garage. Walt Disney and his brother Roy filmed their first project called Alice's Wonderland, which was the first short movie in the Alice Comedies series, in their uncle's garage back in 1923. Apple had its origin in the garage of Steve Jobs' parents.

A college project at Stanford was started in the garage of one Susan Wojcicki and is known to the world today as Google. William Harvey and Arthur Davidson built their first motorcycle in a wooden shed. In 1938, Will Hewlett and Dave Packard started a company in Packard's garage. In 1945, Harold Matson, Ruth, and Elliot Handler started using the leftover material from their picture frame-making company, Mattel to produce dollhouses in a garage. That garage would become the birthplace of the famous doll, Barbie. Michael Dell, too, started from a garage. Nike, meanwhile, had its origin in even humbler surroundings; it began as Blue Ribbon Sports in the trunk of Phil Knight's car.

Garages have played a crucial role in the founding of many successful businesses. The attraction is obvious. There is no rent to pay! However, leaving aside the humor, it is the enterprising desire that shines through in these endeavors. Jeff Bezos has recounted how he pitched his idea of Amazon to his boss. He tried to explain to his boss why he wanted to leave the cushy comfort of his well-paid job and take the risk of becoming an entrepreneur. Bezos has remarked how his boss told him that Amazon was a brilliant idea for someone without a job and not for someone with a job. But Bezos was confident of his venture and commenced it anyway from his garage.

There are enough stories of how these businesses have succeeded and the trials and tribulations they have faced. But I am here to tell you a uniquely Indian story. This is the story of *Saivana* and how we encountered various difficulties negotiating the myriad hues and landscapes of Indian settings. There are several landscapes in the Indian business setting: bureaucratical, legal, societal, etc. Each of them presented its own problems that required negotiations. I failed in some and succeeded in others. This is my journey as an entrepreneur.

The story of *Saivana* can also be traced to a garage. The year was 1994. The garage at my familial home was relatively empty. There was no car, and it was generally used as a storage unit. It was also used for various other purposes.

It was used as a comic book store and even as a reading club venue in my childhood. It was a strange time in those days when a lot of houses had garages but no cars. Maruti was just coming into its own. However, the story of *Saivana* cannot be recounted before I talk about Vandana.

I mentioned in the previous chapter that I had returned to India after graduating from BSL. I had found a job with Dalmia Brothers, an Indian conglomerate run by one of India's oldest business families. Although I did regard my employment as one of the good positive events in my life at that time, I was faced with an entirely different proposition on the personal front. My mother was pressuring me to get married. I was a little too touchy on the subject of marriage.

The first issue was that I could not just think of marriage without my father's presence. The second issue was that I had considered marriage to a girl not so long ago. When I was studying in Drew, I used to come back to India during my holidays. It was on one such visit that I met this beautiful girl at a cards table. It was an uncanny feeling and a reminder of every Bollywood cliché. I knew I was going to marry that girl. She would introduce herself as Vandana. It was the beginning of a roller-coaster relationship. We had to be careful when we went out on dates.

She came from a conservative family. We had to be especially careful of her brother. However, it all came to naught when we had to break up due to the distance between USA and India. So, I was a bit iffy toward the idea of marriage. But my mother was insistent that I get married. It was at this point that there was a marriage proposal and someone came inquiring if my family were amenable to marriage. It must have been a quirk of fate as the girl was Vandana.

My mother had no inkling that Vandana and I had dated, and I for one was secretly thrilled that there was a wedding proposal from her family. But there was a glitch; I had to pass muster with her father and her brother Sudhir (Sudhir plays a very important role later in the book). I still remember Vandana (Vandy) calling me and giving me a briefing on what questions her dad was going to ask me.

Sure enough, when they came to see me, her adorable Dad shot the first question, "What sports do you play?" My father-in-law has been an avid sportsman all his life and an active member of both the Delhi Golf Club and the Delhi Gymkhana Club. Since I knew the questions, I already was prepared with the answers and he was very pleased with my answers. In his book, a sportsman was quite suitable for his daughter, although I should confess that my answers to him were highly exaggerated. Do not get me wrong; whilst in school and college, I was an avid sportsman, from table tennis to cricket to soccer, etc. It is just that once I was in Switzerland, I had no time for any sports. Anyway, one thing led to another, and the supposedly arranged marriage (I am saying arranged from a parent's perspective) was fixed and we got married. It was a bittersweet moment: I was very happy that I was marrying my college sweetheart but at the same time I was bitter because my father was not there.

In 1994, I was newly married and was working in an Indian corporate entity because I wanted to see how decision-making took place in a proper Indian company. If my father would have remained alive, I probably would not have returned to India. I had a job offer from Philip Morris in Hong Kong and I was going to sell cigarettes all my life (at that time I used to smoke a lot). But now I was working in India. Although things were moving along smoothly, a voice within me made me realize I was not all that happy. I hated answering to a superior; I wanted to be my boss. As far as decision-making in the Indian corporate setup was concerned, it was very simple: it was either the Boss's way or the Highway. If your boss was in a good mood, you had a good day, but God forbid if he/she had fought with their spouse that day; even hell would be considered a more pleasant place to park yourself in for the day.

There is a famous joke along these lines. The story goes that a manager invited his team lead and developer out to have lunch. They went to a relatively expensive restaurant and had a good lunch. The manager was famous for being overbearing and shifted a few of his responsibilities to the other two. While they nodded and accepted the responsibilities, they were incensed.

It would amount to added work hours and unnecessary stress for them. However, they had no choice. They stepped out of the restaurant and saw a gift shop. One of the available items looked like an ancient oil lamp. The project lead stepped forward and rubbed it imitating the story of Aladdin. But lo! A genie did come out of the lamp. The genie said, "The custom is that I grant three wishes. But here, in front of me, I have the three of you. So, I will grant you a wish each." The project lead was the first one out of the gate. He wanted to rid himself of the additional work pressures imposed by his boss. He said, "I want to be the first to make a wish. I want to be in Australia and dive and observe the coral reefs without a care in the world." The genie said, "Done." The project lead disappeared. The developer was shocked. She said, "I want to be in Hawaii. I want to be sipping on an endless supply of Pina Coladas without a worry in the world." The genie granted her wish. The boss was displeased. He looked at the genie and said, "I want them both back in the office in 10 minutes." The boss has great control and I did not like that one bit.

This was too much for me. It was the same for my wife. She too acutely felt the problem of being stuck in a corporate job. We both were working at 9-to-5 jobs. A 9-to-5 job can be tedious as it is built along the lines of the industrial revolution. You are paid an 'x' amount of money for the 'x' number of hours you put in. Henry Ford may have mechanized factories with the assembly line production, but almost every job has seen similar mechanization. You punch in your time card when you start work and punch out at the end of the day. But we are not machines. There is not much scope for creativity within your work unless you fashion a new ruse to keep time! Today, with the advent of biometrics, such shenanigans are also not possible. That was another drawback in my 9-to-5 work schedule. I always had to answer to someone, and I often found this strict hierarchy to be irksome. I knew I had to get out.

The daily grind of a 9-to-5 job can also destroy the gears of your creativity and spirit. But I was working in an institution that expected me to do certain tasks for no rhyme or reason.

The only thing that was remotely metrical was its repetition. I had to get out of there and do something else. But do what? I mean, this will always remain a perplexing question for most young people. What to do? There was no concept of start-ups back then. People had barely heard of Infosys or TCS and there was no tech revolution happening in India at that time. Sure, the economy was being liberalized, but it had no impact on my decision-making. One day, I mustered the courage and handed in the my only the last resignation letter in my life. My boss was astounded. He screamed and railed at me that he considered himself my mentor and that I was doing the wrong thing. My family was aghast. "This boy has gone mad" was all they could say.

Saivana is a garment exporting business based out of New Delhi. Before we explore this story further, I want to answer a few quick questions. Why did I choose a garment exporting business instead of, say, hospitality or any other business? Fashion is one of the easier industries to step into and thrive in. My wife, Vandana, was among the graduates of the first batch to pass out of the Pearl Academy of Fashion.

My wife, too, was subjected to a daily grind, and we both wanted out. So, we had a conversation. I asked her, "What do you want to do?" She said, "I am good at fashion." I replied, "Oh, I am awesome in marketing" (clearly the Swiss MBA was talking). We decided to pool our efforts together and start a garment export company. Well, we had no other choice as the garage could only hold one business!

But joking aside, let us revisit this statement: Fashion is one of the easier industries to step into and thrive in. Some of you may have the fundamental question: How? To start in the fashion business, all you need is a sewing machine and a one-car garage. The capital investment is marginal. You could scale up your operations with every successful order. Perhaps, if you have been part of any Resident Welfare Association WhatsApp chat group of your society or apartment complex, you would have come across people who would advertise their tailoring skills and their charges. These could be for ladies' garments, clothes for children, and even suits for men.

There may not be a scientific basis for this, but those will be the most interactive posts within the WhatsApp group if you were to ignore the many forwards of other matters. But why is it that such services can seem so ubiquitous across the country? The answer is simple: most of the homes in our country have a sewing machine. Usually, it is either a Usha or a Singer, or it may be from some other brand as well.

Once my wife and I were struck by the idea of starting a garment company, we first surveyed our site of operations—the garage. We figured that we could position two sewing machines without any problem. We then hired two students from the local fashion school. We asked them to make 60 garments based on my wife's designs. We used all our hard-earned savings for this.

I refused to take money from my relatives. Well, that door was not open anyway; my relatives had made that very clear. Herein, I faced my first challenging landscape. My relatives were dismissive of our plans to start a business. I was told in very clear terms that they did not want me to quit my job, which guaranteed a regular inflow of money. In fact, they had wanted me to be in the civil services. After all, there is no better cushy job in terms of security and payment than a government job.

Essentially, they wanted me to hold a job title that started with I and ended with Services. You get the gist. It was not just for the allure of safety, but because it also held a tag of respectability and stature. I would only realize how those two terms were valued more than what they should have been later on in my life. We shall cover that area in a later chapter.

They were further incensed when they found out that my wife was the sole proprietor of the business. For me, it was a non-issue. What did it matter if the business belonged to me or her? Shouldn't, after marriage, a couple supposed to become one unified front? What belongs to me, belongs to her and vice-versa. Crucially, she was the real brains behind the business who knew what real fashion was about. After all, she had studied at one of the premier institutes of design and understood the fashion industry.

I would be the marketing head to see that her products were sold in the market, but in the end, the first P of marketing is PRODUCT and she knew it better than anyone I knew at that time.

The first logical step we decided on was to go international. India had once been the leading exporter of fine cloth and garments before the British Raj. We thought that we could tap into our ancestral history and become one of the leading exporters from India. There was also one big reason as to why we chose to export. There was NO income tax levied on exports in 1994/1995. What a great incentive that was! Come to think of it, this was probably the first time ever that a macro policy was so applicable in the micro-world.

However, there were a few other issues we needed to address. While there were no taxes to pay, there was the issue of quotas. If you wanted to export garments, you needed to acquire quotas to do so. It was only when we started exporting that we became aware that the cost of each order could vary as quotas had different costs. It was obvious that this process was rife with corruption and severely limited many people from taking up garment exporting. As I experienced this over the past few decades, I can say with relative confidence that it was the quotas that held back India. Look at our neighbors, Pakistan and Bangladesh who had no quotas levied on their exporters. They overtook India when it came to garment exports by 2010. It may come as a surprise, but many businesses made more money by selling quotas than they did from actually exporting their garments! The large garment exporters made more money from this side business than they did from their primary business of exporting garments in the 80s and the 90s. Capitalism can work in mysterious circumstances at times. As a start-up in the 90s, everything was against us. There were no Shark Tanks to pitch our ideas to or angel investors who would help us by putting in seed money. If I were to liken our circumstances to a journey, all the signs we came across said, "Stop and turn around." It looked as if we were hurtling toward a cliff bound for a certain downfall. Even though we were garment exporters, the quotas meant that some choices would not even make it to the discussion table.

22

Some of the goods needed quotas that were prohibitively expensive. So, our choices were limited. However, we were fortunate that some garments did not need quotas. So, we gravitated towards them.

One of the choices that did not require quotas was the export of silk garments. It was the silken lining in what seemed a doomed journey. The point I learned is that even in the most adverse conditions, an opportunity can be spotted.

However, returning to *Saivana*'s story, we had one question: where to start? We decided to go big. We settled on Paris to make our debut as garment exporters. We decided to participate in the Prêt a Porter fair in Paris. It is an apparel and clothing trade show that is still an ongoing fixture today. Neither my wife nor I had ever been to Paris. But we knew that Paris was considered the Mecca of the fashion world. If we had to start somewhere, we would do well to start there.

For the uninitiated, Prêt a Porter means ready-to-wear garments. When we think of the fashion industry, we think of catwalks, models, and designs that boggle our minds. While those are a part of the fashion industry, the shows on the catwalks are known as Haute Couture. They are one-off pieces and not meant for mass production or mass consumption. Prêt a Porter, as the name suggests, is about ready-to-wear garments that can be mass-produced and mass-consumed.

Now that I think of it, once again, the Government of India came to my help. Their premier trade show agency, the Indian Trade Promotion Organisation (ITPO), was taking part in the show, and they were going to have a separate area for Indian exporters at the show. Not only that, they were offering highly subsidized rates for exporters to participate in the show.

Amazingly, first, there were no taxes on garment exports, and now, here was a Government of India agency helping us to take part in one of the world's premier shows. I still remember going into their office to fill up the required forms and the officer looking at me suspiciously.

But, in all fairness, ITPO was definitely a godsend for a first-time exporter. Who says that governments cannot help start-ups? I am a prime example (in other words, Exhibit A) of an entrepreneur who was helped by the government.

However, the trip did not begin on the most auspicious of notes. Just three days before our departure, Vandana decided to show her designs to one of her professors to get a second opinion. The professor was furious when she saw the clothes. She did not consider them good enough for an international show. She bemoaned the fact that Vandana had learned nothing from her.

However, this was too close to the date of the fair and we had already made the necessary payments for our travel and residential stay and the space in the fair. We decided to brave the odds. Vandana was in tears the whole of that evening convinced that our trip was going to be a failure. The professor had totally decimated her collection.

We were flying in blind. You should remember that this was the age of STD and ISD phone booths. The commercialization of the Internet was just beginning to gather steam. So, we had no idea about the logistics of Paris. Our choices were solely driven by cost reduction. We had asked the travel agencies for the cheapest accommodation and booked our hotel rooms accordingly. It turned out to be a big mistake. We landed in Paris, and we got a ride to our hotel. When we had registered ourselves, we asked the concierge about the fair.

We explained to him that we were participating in the fair and wanted to know how we could get there. It was only then we realized that, while booking our accommodation, we had only looked at the prices and not proximity to the fair. We were staying in one of the northern arrondissements of Paris while the fair was being held in one of the southern arrondissements. It would take us three hours to get there. So, we had to take the Paris Metro, dragging the boxes that contained our garments all the way to set up our booth at the fair. We arrived at the venue. We were a bit overwhelmed by the scale of the fair itself.

We could see booths being set up, and even as we moved toward our booth, we could see that we were a tad bit unprepared. Soon we assembled our booth, and I could see that our booth was sparse compared to the others around us. We had a small stall and we organized our garments in it. Only after we had assembled our stall did we realize our inexperience would cost us. We were positioned with our Indian garment exporters due to the ITPO connection, but we were the only rookies. The others were trade-fair veterans and it was clear they knew what they were doing. Their stalls were three to four times the size of ours. We did not even need to check their garments as it was quite clear to us that we were 'David' in this story.

We were truly enlightened to the 'Goliath' nature of the challenge when we saw the other booths lit up with numerous light bulbs and other colorful lights. Our lack of preparation only came to light (no pun intended) as dusk approached and we saw our stall shrouded in darkness. I approached the ITPO guy for more lights and he dismissed me saying we had paid for only two lights and two lights were all we would get. It was a very deflating moment. Instead of excitement, when we saw our stall, we saw our future slipping away. Who would enter a stall that was shrouded in darkness? I tried asking people around for help and advice, but no one gave me a clear answer.

It was at this point that I came upon a solution. I told my wife that I could arrange for lights. When she asked me how I was going to do that, I told her, "Indian Embassy". My thinking was that the Embassy was set up to solve the problems of Indians. So, in my foolhardy way, I went into the Embassy looking for the commercial attache to help us. After all, they are there to facilitate trade between the two nations. Needless to say, I was promptly thrown out of the Embassy. Today I laugh at what I did. I actually walked into the Indian Embassy in Paris asking for help with lights for our nine square feet stall at a fair in Paris. Talk about being naïve! We could not come up with any solution for the lights and soon it was time for the fair to start. We were there for four days. We had people come in and look at our garments in our 3 x 3 feet stall.

We spoke as eloquently as possible. We smiled our brightest smiles. We felt good about ourselves. For our first attempt, we did extremely well. We had managed to have 60 garments sewn in the garage of my home. We had managed to reach Paris and were showcasing ourselves at the world-famous Prêt a Porter fair. We had overcome the challenge of having our hotel three hours away from the fair.

We were the runt of the litter compared to the booths that surrounded us. We had learned that arranging a businessman's lights for a fair is not part of international diplomatic affairs. We were constantly pushed and challenged. But we responded to every challenge and rose to it. We had done extremely well.

Now, the more inquisitive among you will have one question. How many orders did we get from our expedition to Paris? There is no easy way to say this, but we got zero orders. That is not to say we were surprised. We had indications that despite our best efforts, we would be getting the worst result. I knew a bit of French, and when potential clients stepped into the booth, I heard them speak. They did not know that I could speak French. I overheard their comments that the garments were bad. None of them liked it. We were reminded of how aghast Vandana's professor had been when we had first shown her the garments.

So, we returned to New Delhi with a pocketful of visiting cards but no orders. Then we had to face the people who had known that we were going to Paris. We will cover the influence of Delhi and its socialites in a forthcoming chapter. They immediately wanted to know about our Paris adventure. They expected us to be successful. Many of them had nothing else to offer once they knew that we had failed. They expected us to have a business worth Rs 50 lakh from our one visit to Paris. As we sat reflecting, I could not help but remonstrate with myself. I was the marketing and sales guy. Even if the garments were bad, I had to find a way to secure a buyer. It is said that the best salesman can sell ice to the Eskimos. I wanted to be that guy, and I had failed. I believe that you could have the worst product, but you can still find a buyer for it.

It was absolutely inconceivable to us that we returned without bagging even a single order. All kinds of doubts came up in our minds. Maybe the fair selection was wrong, maybe our products were wrong, maybe our prices were too high, and so on. Were we finished before we had even started our lives? How was it that the other Indian exporters were filling up their books with one order after another while we were left twiddling our thumbs in our booth? The fact that my MBA had failed me was a real gut-wrenching thought. Did I have to go back into the job market?

I was sure I definitely would not be able to work in India having tasted a little bit of the Indian corporate experience before we had started *Saivana*. If I had to take up a job then it would have to be outside India. Our time post-Paris was one of the lowest moments of our lives, more so for me, because I felt I had let Vandana down. We had also decided that we would not start a family until we had enough money. And then we decided we were not ready to give up! We were going to give it one more try, but this time we had to get it right. There could be no margin for error (okay, that is a corny line) but our lives were at stake here. We were definitely not ready to give up. After a bit of soul-searching, both my wife and I knew that we had to do it right. So, we decided to take another chance. But we had blown our savings away on the first trip. My relatives were certainly not very encouraging. We had become estranged over the fact that I was ready to take the risk again.

There was also a certain sense of pride in me that did not allow me to approach Vandana's parents for support. My father would have slapped me from the grave if I had gone to Vandana's parents asking for money. This was not the school I was from. But I had a few good friends. They pitched in to help, believing in our dream. They asked no questions but just reposed their trust in me and believed that I would repay them. It was with their money that we bought the flight tickets to Paris. We were a year older, but we were also wiser. We were more experienced. That is not to say we were now Goliath. We were still David, but we had the slingshot ready this time around!

27

We booked a hotel next to the fair grounds. We were more confident. There were no trips to the Embassy for additional lights. The stall still measured the same: 3 x 3 feet. But this time, our modus operandi was different. The previous year, both of us had stayed in our stall awaiting clients. This time Vandana sat in the stall, while I went around the fair looking for clients.

My goal was to look for designers and offer the services of *Saivana* to manufacture their designs. This was the year 1995. India had a notorious reputation when it came to garment exports. Some would even say that this legacy endures to this day. But at that moment, India was infamous when it came to garment exports. The cloth used was always of poor quality. And to top it, the Indians were known to be always late (the universal Indian Standard Time). For these reasons, India was not considered a reliable source for garment manufacturing. Thus, India was battling a twin perception problem: bad quality garments and always being late.

So, when I went visiting these stalls, I had to battle this twin stigma. However, I was prepared. I had my own version of an elevator pitch. I was met with the same response every time. People told me that Indians had no sense of time and were not reliable. I countered by saying, "I know we can't design for the Frenchwoman while we are sat in the backroads of Delhi. I only ask you to come to our stall and look at our samples. Ignore the designs, but look at the quality of our work, be it in the materials used or in the caliber of the stitching work. I can assure you that they will meet your standards."

A few of them did take me up on the offer and came to inspect our wares. They were very complimentary of our samples. It was soon nearing the end of the fair, and we still had no order on our table. We received interest and curiosity but, crucially, no orders. It was extremely disheartening as we saw the other Indian stalls all around us book innumerable orders based on their samples.

One of the "aunties" from a neighboring stall even came up to us and informed us that we were in the wrong trade and offered Vandana a job in her company. This was extremely perplexing.

On one hand, she said we were not meant for this line of work, but on the other hand, she was offering my wife a job in her company (I know the company well but surely will not disclose their name. I am sure she meant well). This remark of hers actually served to encourage us and lifted our spirits. It was just a matter of getting the first order.

Forget throwing stones like David, we were left swatting flies in our stall. On the final day, an Indian woman walked into our stall. She told us, "You have some good stuff here." She must have seen our faces brighten as she immediately clarified, "Listen, I am not a buyer. But my brother is a businessman. He has two boutiques in Paris. He will definitely be interested in placing an order with you people. Please go show him your samples." I told her that as the fair was ending on that day, we could visit him the next day. She was amenable to that and gave us his address. That night, after the fair ended, we again went into a depression.

Again, zero was the net result. Yes, we fielded a lot of inquiries but not a single firm order. We had received more inquiries compared to what we received in the first fair but they remained just that, inquiries. We were now dependent on an address given to us by a stranger. It was the longest night of our lives. If we did not get an order the next day, *Saivana* was finished. The dream was over and we would have to choose a different path. I still remember walking with Vandana next to the Eiffel Tower that night, each of us silent as we knew the end was near.

We again had failed miserably. The next day we packed all our samples and dragged those samples across the streets of Paris to the address given to us by that lady. We could not find a taxi due to some strike in Paris at the time and we had to walk. It was a long walk, struggling with the three suitcases full of samples. Finally, we reached the store.

We were met by an elderly gentleman named Mr. Vally. He was from Pondicherry and had been living in Paris for decades. He owned two boutiques and they were both called Indira (the other boutique was across the street and was run by his wife).

He looked at our samples and was happy. He placed an order for around French Francs 15300 or USD 3060 at the time. We were elated. How many of you remember your first salary? Do you remember the sense of exultation? We felt the same, but with greater intensity. We had an order resulting from our efforts. It was one of the greatest feelings I have ever experienced. Somebody out there believed in our talents. We had spent so much money and energy and carted our samples across the world twice. Finally, someone acknowledged it and placed an order.

Order number SE-001/95 was finally written down by us. I think my hand was shaking as I took down the order while Vandana showed him our samples. The total order was for 150 pieces. Wow! It was incredible. I mentally calculated we would make at least $1800 as net profit.

However, we came across an immediate problem. I had read up on export and import from one of the bulky textbooks available then. These textbooks or tomes were so big that they could double up as pillows if you wanted to sleep in class. But I had brushed up on the terms, conditions, and legalities involved in the export business, anticipating a rush of orders. My inexperience would reveal itself when the man asked how we wanted our payment. Much like a book-smart academic, I said, "Yes, we would like an irrevocable letter of credit."

Fortunately, I relied on myself when it came to documentation. One of the most critical aspects of international trade is documentation. I did not rely on anyone else to teach me the ins and outs. I ensured that I would never be caught up in a lack of knowledge. I could be misled by others or there could be a case where someone else also would not know the full extent of a particular law. Ignorance of the law does not portray a businessman in good light.

I had to rely on myself to learn all about business and the laws that govern it. Nabhi Publishers had produced an 800-page tome about export documentation. This book was my primary reference, and I used to read it every day.

I must have cross-checked with that book on each step as I processed different orders. What is a bill of lading? What is a bill of exchange? If you want to enter the game, you need to know the rules of the game. International trade is not just about garments or products.

However, Mr. Vally looked bemused as no one gave an irrevocable letter of credit for an order of just $3060. But he was gracious and accepted it. We were excited, and as I said, we felt an elevated sense of excitement akin to that felt when receiving our first ever salaries.

Perhaps it is why we were also equally extra insensitive with our first revenue, which we still had not earned a single penny of, and wanted to celebrate. So, we took the next flight out to New York to celebrate with a few friends and some of Vandana's cousins.

Unsurprisingly, we ended up spending more than our projected revenue. Note to budding entrepreneurs: DO NOT spend more than you have earned and certainly DO NOT SPEND anything BEFORE you have earned it. We then returned to India and immediately encountered a few problems. The problem with overspending when you run a business is that you will run into financial troubles sooner rather than later. You do not have an assured monthly source of refill like a salary. So, you cannot even scrimp and save in the final days of the month hoping your salary would arrive the next week. I have to stress, once more, the importance of having friends on this journey when your own relatives have deserted you. It was my friends who stepped up once more. They loaned me money. No, loaning would be the wrong word because a loan implies interest charged. These friends just gave the money to me without asking any questions.

One of them, in particular, was Sanjay Khanna, my childhood friend and the scion of Kailash Nath Associates. One day, I had no money to pay the salary of my workers. I went to Sanjay's office and he saw how troubled I was. Without saying anything, he just handed me his credit card and said "I have Rs. 60,000 in the account and you can withdraw from the nearest ATM on this card."

Who does that today? Mind you, he was answerable for all his expenses to his grandfather, of whom I was very scared since my kindergarten days at St. Columba's (Sanjay and I had gate-crashed a wedding that was being held in front of his house to have a soft drink. We were kids and were just being naughty. No one caught us and we came out of the wedding giggling. But his grandfather found out and the next day, both of us got resounding well-deserved slaps for doing so from him. That ended our marriage gate-crashing careers). Sanjay trusted me blindly and encouraged me to dare. This is why *"Zindagi mein yeh dost zaroori hota hai"*: The friend who will always have your back.

The first few years of *Saivana* were all about making garments out of antique silk saris procured from the by-lanes of Old Delhi through street hawkers. We would buy these old silk sarees, cut them, and fashion patchwork silk jackets and blouses out of them. Our second customer was a boutique shop in Sloane Square in London and they loved our 'antique' pieces. I think for the first three to four years of *Saivana*, we only made those garments. It was funny how we started making a name for ourselves amongst the street hawkers of Janpath and Old Delhi. They knew that if old saris could be procured from the villages, they had a ready buyer in us. It did not matter if the sari was even tattered, there was a buyer and it was *Saivana Exports*.

If I were to distill my experiences and condense them into a few bite-sized inputs, these are the ones I would want to share with you, dear reader. If you want to succeed as an entrepreneur, operate in an area where you are the king. Do not start a business with just the idea of getting away from a 9-to-5 job. Find out where your genius and enterprise lie. It is the place where your interests, skills, and passions align. Francesc Miralles and Hector Garcia identify this area as the Ikigai. At *Saivana*, there was a perfect amalgamation when it came to Vandana and me. Vandana's genius lay in the domain of fashion. I can say without any doubt that *Saivana* could only become the force it is today because of her. She is technically proficient in the area and our customers have come to rely on her. She can understand and speak in their language.

Her technical expertise when it comes to fabrics, stitching techniques, and accessories is second to none. It has meant that she becomes the gate that welcomes our customers and provides a great comfort zone for them. She also becomes the bulwark when it comes to potential fraudulent customers and scammers.

Some husbands may be jealous of their wife's capabilities and success. However, I am not bound by any such petty masculine pride. My source of pride, however, lay in my wife. I knew she was the fulcrum around which the entire company revolved. She was the most valuable asset of the company.

However, this was a double-edged sword as she was also the biggest liability of the company. If she were to be absent for a few days, it would hurt *Saivana*. Over the years, I have tried to reduce the reliance *Saivana* had on her. I have hired the most technically proficient pattern masters in the NCR region. It is here that I have to stress how remarkable she is in her area of expertise. The pattern masters I hired may have come from the most prestigious training programs with knowledge of the latest trends.

But they are not a patch on her. They still fall short when it comes to Vandana and her prodigious knowledge. She may have passed out of the famed Pearl Academy. But her experience and knowledge did not come from the classroom.

It was the fruit of her painstaking efforts and time spent on the shop floor. She worked with pattern masters and in most cases, taught them how to correct mistakes in a pattern. A pattern is the most important aspect of a garment. Pattern masters always listened to what Vandana had to say. She was always right.

There have been times some pattern masters may have different ideas and have discussed them with her. Those discussions have only shown how right Vandana had been. Those discussions remind me of a famous football manager by the name of Brian Clough. He was in his pomp in the late 60s and the next decade. He was charismatic and was a brilliant manager. One day he was posed a question about what he did when some players raised doubts about his knowledge and coaching.

What would he do if they said they ought to do it in some other way? He charmingly answered that he would listen to them and then they would have a conversation about why he was right. While Vandana may not make the same remark, I have been witness to several discussions which concluded that Vandana's judgment and insight were the correct methods.

One of the best indicators that *Saivana* and Vandana were the best choice came from the trust we earned. Our buyers knew that they could trust Vandana to make the right call. Our two visits to the Prêt a Porter had not shaken her. She was made of sterner and more passionate stuff.

She worked harder to let her talent shine. I have always prided myself on my work ethic. But when I see Vandana, I feel that I am not as hardworking and passionate. It was her passion and hardwork that propelled *Saivana* to new heights.

I have never seen a more hardworking person than her. She would work till the wee hours of the morning. She could be working on the costing of 300 possible styles. Our dining table would be full of files that Vandana used to bring home to work on.

Her hard work ensured that our clients learned to trust her and her decisions. It was also apparent to our buyers that they had to speak to Vandana regarding their designs and styling. They had full confidence and still hold the same confidence in her. She would also communicate with the buyers about what could be wrong with their styles or possible areas of enhancing their current styles. This style may not work. This color may not work. A particular styling may not work as it may not be production-friendly. That trust was a huge boost for *Saivana*. It was understood by the buyers that as long as Vandana is looking into the styles, they had no worries. They knew that the task would be executed flawlessly. What solutions could be found? Over time, they started to trust her input. They came to trust her judgment calls. Delivering products in a timely fashion builds trust. We delivered our orders on time. Our buyers knew that we could deliver the goods. However, they also knew that they could rely and trust us on quality.

We had overturned the infamy that had attached itself to us due to the mere reason that we were Indians. Vandana spent time on the shop floor engaged in the process. She learned what worked and what did not. She could speak to clients and tell them of possible solutions. This is important. Vandana did not just raise problems. She would have a few possible solutions as well. Her interactions with clients only broadened her perspective. She began to learn what worked elsewhere.

Our clients could be based in Paris. They could be based elsewhere in Europe and later even in America. She learned the nuances and fine details. Her experience on the shop floor made her aware of the situation at ground zero. She was able to synergize these seemingly different points to produce the best possible products. Buyers started respecting the calls that were being taken in New Delhi.

I cannot stress this enough; it is vital that you operate from a place of strength. When you operate from that place, you can set the rules and play the game on your terms. If you are dictated to in terms of just revenue making, you will only march to the beat of another's drum. Vandana, in the beginning, worked from a zone of talent and genius. The first two visits to Paris showed her the possible shortcomings. I am reminded of a Maya Angelou quote that said, *"Do the best you can until you know better. Then when you know better, do better."* She worked hard to fill the gaps in her knowledge. She worked tirelessly to know the trends and techniques followed abroad. She wanted to find how to translate it across to her shop floor. She did so by trying it out herself first. Most people may find it daunting and look to others for help. Bur Vandana knew that she had to lead from the front.

It was not about being a leader. She wanted to be at the top of the game. She knew if she had to explain the details to the staff on the shop floor, she could only do it if she knew how to do it first. Her genius and talent shone through when she was able to come up with the solutions and explain them to her staff. It is in those interactions that she made herself aware of the ground realities.

If you want to be a successful entrepreneur, it is critical that you make your area of genius and talent, an area of extreme strength. It is not enough to be good at something. You have to tune your physical and mental faculties to align with your expertise, talent, and passion. Vandana's passion lay in fashion. However, it is her drive that made her look past the two visits to Paris. She wanted to be the best at her skill. She took no shortcuts. If it meant working late into the night, it did not faze her. She shed any shred of conceited pride at the door. It was not enough for her to be good at it. She had graduated from the Pearl Academy of Fashion, a premier institute. Her talent and skill were not in doubt. So, she worked on making her talent her strength.

Today, she can look at a garment and tell you the cost. She can tell you how much fabric was used on average to produce it. She can tell you the stitching technique. She is a virtuoso, and she is like Serena Williams dominating tennis courts across the world grass at Wimbledon or a Simone Biles in gymnastics. Think of any great exponent in any field, Vandana can hold her ground when it comes to fashion. She is the best when it comes to fabrics and garments.

If you are not sure where your strength lies, I encourage you to discover it. Be curious and find that out. Do you remember how we were as children? We are inordinately curious. When our parents warned us not to touch fire, we had to touch to find out why we were so warned. Somewhere along the way, we lose that curiosity. We become cowed down by our fears. Push back your fears and explore. I am not asking you to touch the fire again. I just want you to kindle the fire of curiosity and find out where your genius lies if you want to be a successful entrepreneur. I am sure you have heard of the adage 'fortune favors the bold.' So, be bold and be curious.

On a related note, I want to address the importance of failures. If you were to look at our two visits to Paris and the Prêt a Porter, they could be seen as failures. However, it is important to bounce back from the failure. I went around the fair the second time we were there hoping to find customers. It is one of the most important lessons in marketing and sales.

Learn to speak for your business and product. If you are hungry, you need to make a statement to others that you are hungry. If your mouth is closed, then food cannot be an option. It is why I went around the fair hoping to land a client. If you sit around waiting for good things to happen, it will not come. You need to put in the effort. Luck will follow. Some people may feel uncomfortable with this approach for a variety of reasons.

But you need to push beyond your limits. We become uncomfortable when we are faced with the prospect of failure. So, we choose to stay in our comfort zones. You can only grow when you push beyond what you consider to be discomfort. You can hone your competitive edge only when you grow past your comfort zone. Become comfortable with your discomfort and not your seemingly safe zone. What is the worst that can happen?

People may say no; however, nothing has changed. But what if they say yes? I was able to persuade more than a few people to visit our stall by asking them. They looked past the stigma and came to my stall because I asked them to. I do not think we could have had that many people visit our stall if I had not put in the effort to ask them.

It is vital that entrepreneurs do not let their failures dictate terms. It is critical that they develop a high tolerance level. Some of the greatest triumphs were snatched from the jaws of utter failure. If you want to be a successful entrepreneur, do not play safe. My dreams and Vandana's dreams were big; so, we never even entertained the thought of playing small. We went to Prêt a Porter as a first-time exporter. Of course, our inexperience showed, especially during our first visit. However, we learned from those experiences. The first visit could have made us afraid. There were feelings of disappointment when we returned from our first visit. However, neither of us was afraid of going back again. We knew we had the capability to become a reputed garment exporter. It is imperative that one does not cultivate a mindset of fear. Most people fear stepping into the unknown. They are besieged by worry and doubts. Wandering minds become the devil's vacation spot.

We must understand that life is a collection of random and chaotic events. One must aspire to become like the monster from Greek mythology, Hydra. When one of its heads is cut off, two more will spring in its place. Paris became the crucible in which our mentalities were forged. Our first order from Indira vouched for our efforts. We have never looked back since. However, there are bound to be growing problems that one has to meet and counter.

It is the case when it comes to any budding enterprise. The next problem occurred when my mother objected to the business running from the garage.

She did not want strangers coming into the garage to work. We had to move out. However, we knew that we had to move out anyway. The garage could only hold two sewing machines, and we needed more machines to execute our first order. We then found a place in Tughlaqabad in the outskirts of Delhi. It would be our new factory and the base of operations for *Saivana* for the near future.

Extra customization

- Paris was certainly very enlightening. If you ask me about the tourist spots and the romance of the city, I am afraid I will not have much to tell you. Champs-Élysées is a good spot and one of the best sights. As you know, our two trips to Paris were not exactly the greatest return on investment. France can be a challenging place to navigate, and it was certainly not made easier by my poor French. However, our two trips to the Prêt a Porter fair would be the only two times we went to a fair as *Saivana*. We may not have had the greatest start, but we built on those efforts to become what we are today. Today, we have even left many of the seemingly successful business stalls in those fairs far behind us in terms of growth and revenue. There were people from those neighboring stalls who could not help but gloat over their large number of bookings even as we sat despondently. However, today we have become a bigger success.

- So, expect setbacks when you start a business. No one is going to be a success from the first strike. You will be extremely lucky if you do, but becoming a successful business involves more than luck. It is about perseverance even when many people dissuade you. How do you face failure? Know that it is a part and parcel of this endeavor. It will never be easy.

So, once you have decided to become an entrepreneur, be ready to fail. And more importantly, be prepared to pick yourself up and persevere. What if we had never gone back to Paris for the second time?

"The best way to predict the future is to create it."

- Peter Drucker

3
THE MOSQUITO SOUFFLÉ

"Customs inspectors could not stop the export of software through telephone lines; labour inspectors could not stop software engineers from talking to customers in America at night; excise inspectors could not harass the IT firms because the government did not levy tax on services. Much like Gurgaon, India's knowledge economy literally grew at night when the government slept."
— Gurcharan Das, India Grows At Night

My family had asked us to move our business from the garage as they planned to buy another vehicle. It was a polite way of conveying the message that they wanted us out. We were left with no choice. We did not know where to go and had to explore our options. We were on a limited budget, and we also knew that we had to increase our workforce to meet the demands of our first order. We needed people to serve in different roles. We needed tailors and also people who could iron the finished garments. We estimated that we needed ten people.

So, we had to look for a space that could accommodate ten people. We also had to figure in some extra space in case there was a need to expand in the near future. These were some of the factors we had to consider over the primary factor of cost.

We were running on borrowed funds, and we had to budget for salaries and the rent for such a space. Vandana and I scoured many possible sites, but we could not find any suitable ones. It was in this quest that we came to Tughlaqabad. When you read this name, the first image that comes to your mind will probably be that of the Tughlaqabad fort. This is a fort built by Ghiyas-Ud-Din Tughlaq, the founder of the Tughlaq dynasty. It was abandoned in 1327 and is now in a dilapidated state. Perhaps, we saw a similar image when we arrived at Tughlaqabad: a scene of abandonment and dilapidation. It seemed like the city development authorities had totally overlooked this area.

Tughlaqabad was not exactly an industrial zone. It was more like a village in the midst of a city. But it had none of the urban finesse or advantages. The roads were filled with potholes, and some of them were not even paved completely. There were open drains that flanked the roads. And the ever-present stench let you know that these drains were not cleaned regularly. There were places where the sewers overflowed.

There were many areas that had stagnant water. These were ripe breeding grounds for mosquitos. You may perhaps think that this chapter was named Mosquito Souffle because of these conditions. We shall visit the true reason soon. But we found a place in Tughlaqabad that met all our requirements. The cleanliness and conditions were not ideal.

Vandana and I decided that we would try to control only those matters that we could do something about. If the surroundings were not ideal, we would at least keep our factory spick and span. We would provide the best working conditions for our workforce. We could control that aspect. Healthy working conditions would only lead to healthy, productive work. Thus, we moved from the garage to a matchbox-like factory in Tughlaqabad. The factory was small, but it was big enough for our work. We quickly set about working to fulfill our first order. We were determined not to cause any delay from our end. We wanted to ensure that the faith reposed in us was justified. We worked with a lot of energy.

A few days after we had opened our factory, a man walked into our building. He was dressed in a wrinkled checked shirt and trousers. He had a hawkish air about him. He glared at us over the rims of his spectacles. You could even smell the beedi he had been smoking from some meters away.

He said in a loud voice that he wished to meet with the person in charge. I walked up to him and introduced myself as Rajat. He peered at me and said, "I have come to inspect the factory." I was taken aback. I was not aware of any inspections, and I had not received any notice regarding any such inspections. I was immediately suspicious of this person.

He could be a thief who had come to scope out the factory. I was not very sure of his credentials. He had not introduced himself and had just declared that he was here for an inspection; I was incensed. I asked him, "Who the hell are you? What have you come to inspect?" My anger and questions triggered an equivalent reaction. He said in an equally irate tone, "I am the health inspector. I have to come to inspect your premises for mosquito breeding grounds."

The open door of the factory carried the smells from the adjacent open sewers and drains into the factory. Before I go on with this story, I probably should tell you a bit about my background. I had studied very little in India at the famous St. Columba's (yes Shah Rukh Khan's alma mater) until my seventh grade. I then spent the next five years in Manila, Philippines.

This was followed by the infamous days at Drew and then my stay in Switzerland for my MBA. This meant I had never been exposed to such an environment and here I was now, in a heated argument with a supposed sanitation and health inspector in Tughlaqabad.

There were a lot of mosquitos outside and an open environment that encouraged their growth. However, that did not seem to bother him, but he seemed inordinately interested in my factory. I asked him politely to show me his credentials. I wanted to see his identity card. But he was incensed by that question. He shouted, "You dare ask for my ID? Who are you? Don't you know how business works?

Have some common sense, man. I am the health inspector. You have to take my word for it."

I was unmoved. I insisted that he show me his ID card. He erupted in anger and promised me that I would pay for this action. I had had enough and asked my watchman to kick him out. His eyes widened in disbelief and he stormed out. I turned back to the work floor.

I could see my employees were shocked, and there were even expressions of pity on some of their faces. I was a bit surprised. However, I would know the reason only a couple of days later. I received an envelope via registered post. I signed the sheet and received it.

I opened it and realized the price I had to pay for my outburst. It was a summons from the court. I was given a date and was asked to present myself at the court at 9 am. When I looked for the reason, it stated that I had refused to show my premises to a health/sanitary inspector from the local municipal corporation. I was shocked.

It quickly wore off as the day passed. I had been part of many debate teams during my school and college years. I knew how to present cogent arguments and had won many competitions. I knew that I could successfully present my perspective to the court and get out of this pickle.

There were a few days left for the court appointment. I prepared a speech. If I could have patted myself on the back, I would have done it. I thought it was one of my better efforts. My workers did not share my enthusiasm. They told me that I would be penalized regardless. I was sure that I would surprise them instead.

This was the month of May, and Delhi can be unforgiving. Temperatures can soar up to 40 to 45 degrees Celsius. I was keen to make an impression in court. I was dressed in an immaculate white shirt and a pair of black trousers.

I then completed the ensemble with a stylish blazer and necktie. I looked the part of an outstanding businessman. I drove my car to the court premises. I was there nice and early. I had reached at 8:45 am.

There were fifteen more minutes for my assigned time, and I expected that the proceedings would be completed by 10 am or, at the latest, by 11 am. I stepped out, and the heat hit me immediately. I went to one of the clerks and produced my summons.

I was assigned a number. As I wondered about the number, I was informed that I could step into the court when my number was called. My lack of knowledge regarding these matters was becoming clear to me. My number was in three digits. However, I still expected to finish by lunchtime. I stood in a line to see the speed of the process. I saw the line move rapidly. I was encouraged and even assumed that by 11 am, my number would be called.

The heat, however, was already affecting me. My blazer did not help me either. My collar was already damp and I was sweating buckets. I decided it would be better if I waited in the car. I was able to see the queue from where I had parked my car. So, I seated myself in the car and waited for the line to move.

As the morning wore on, the heat was getting more intense. There was not even a remote waft of breeze to bring me some relief and cool me down. I had bought a newspaper, and I used it as a hand fan. I kept waving it to find some relief. It felt heaven-sent. But eventually, my arms cramped up in pain, and I had to stop. I knew that I could only do so in intervals. Unfortunately, the line seemed to be moving at a snail's pace.

It was soon 11 am. The line had barely moved, and the heat seemed to be even more unforgiving. I had already removed my blazer, an action that only afforded me marginal relief. My shirt was drenched in sweat. I thought of having lunch, but I was reluctant to move. There were no restaurants nearby, and I did not want to miss my number in the queue due to hunger.

It was 12 noon. The sun was at its apex, and my hands were aching from waving the newspaper-fashioned fan. There were now flies buzzing about, which was adding to my irritation. I regretted not having brought some snacks along with me. One hour later, I stepped out of the car. My water bottle was empty and I was looking to refill it. Luckily, there was a water tap within the court premises.

I filled the bottle and saw that the line had not moved for over 30 minutes. On inquiring, I was told that the court was in recess as it was lunchtime for the judge. I was stumped, and no one was even able to provide me an accurate time when the judge could return.

An errant thought struck me that maybe some of these waiting people would leave the queue to go have their lunch and would be delayed in getting back. A happy thought! My turn may just come sooner than anticipated. I was further reassured when a nearby clerk announced that the judge was returning to the courtroom.

I was mistaken. Another hour passed, and I was still in my car. But the line seemed to be moving faster. At 2:30 pm, I saw that the line had sufficiently progressed for me to join the queue. I stepped out of my car and having shown my number, joined the line. It was when I joined the line that I understood my lack of foresight. Many of these people had brought packed lunches from their homes.

The temperature had not dropped. The rivulets of sweat that poured down my back were making new design patterns on my already damp shirt. I realized people could see through my translucent white shirt. I had to bear with it. The blazer could have hidden the sight, but I could take not take the risk of putting it on as staying cool was the priority now. I assumed that I would be called in an hour. What do you think happened?

Well, no luck once again. Two hours passed, and it was 4:30 pm, and my number had not yet been called. Mercifully, when the clock struck 4:45 pm, my number was finally called. I wore my blazer and stepped into the courtroom. I mentally revised the points of my speech. There are many movies and television series that show courtroom dramas. These images will be shattered when you step into a courtroom, especially the civil courts in India. The courtroom was surreal. It was a small room.

There was a judge and a man with a weathered face who sat with open briefcases full of cash; these held the daily fine collections. The courtroom was on the premises of the Delhi Water Board. The other defendants were people who operated illegal shops and kiosks and pushcart vendors.

They did not have licenses to operate and thus had to pay fines. They were in regular everyday clothes. Then there was me, an entrepreneur with an MBA from Switzerland, who was bedecked in the finest western attire, albeit drenched in sweat. I had heard the previous fines being imposed as I awaited my turn.

They were generally in the denominations of 100, 150, and 200. A fine collector was collecting the cash from the defendants. My case number was announced, and the judge looked at me and asked, "Guilty or not guilty?"

I was once more disabused of my notions of a courtroom based on what was popularly shown on the screen. Yet, I persisted. I said, "Your honor! The person..." I was planning to start with my strongest point that the inspector refused to show me his credentials. But the loud sound of the judge came barreling back, "Guilty or not guilty?" I froze at his anger. I was cowed, and in a timid voice, I said, "Guilty." The judge immediately told me that the fine was Rs 6000. That was a princely amount in those days. A collective gasp went around the courtroom. It was the highest fine to be levied that day.

I was shocked. I could not believe my ears. I had been there from 9 am, and at the end of the day, I was poorer by Rs 6000. Why? Because I had refused to show my factory to an inspector who would not show me his ID!

It was a painful lesson. Somehow, I borrowed the money and paid the fine. But it was a very important lesson for me. I learned that I had to navigate through all these statutory inspections on this journey. I had not just lost Rs 6000/-. I had also lost an entire day. I could have done something to add value; instead, I was left kicking my heels at a courthouse.

I immediately realized that this was going to be a very difficult journey. The mosquito inspector came once more, four days later. This time I had to let him in. He did not show me his ID this time either. However, I had '6000' reasons to believe him now. He inspected the factory and said that there were mosquitos inside the premises and fined me. I had another court visit scheduled. I had learned my lesson from my previous visit.

I asked one of my employees to go in my stead. An idea struck me, and I asked him to wear tattered clothes when he visited the court and ask for mercy. He was not to wear clothes that conveyed a perception of being well-off. He followed my instructions and he was subjected to the same process. The judge asked him, "Guilty or not guilty?" He answered, "Guilty." He also pleaded for forgiveness.

The judge saw his attire and appearance and fined us Rs 500. I realized appearances matter. I would be further educated on that lesson later in my life. I knew that I had to send my employees in similar clothing styles from now on for any court appearances. However, this only angered the inspector even further. He could see that we were paying fines continuously, but he was not receiving any of them. He came 24 times in total over the next four months. I was fined after every visit.

He cajoled and berated me on every visit. He claimed that I had no idea how to run a business and called me stupid. I thought there was a problem with the operations. I checked and double-checked. I could not find any problems. I was too inexperienced to realize that the inspector was after his share. It is only with hindsight that I understood his remark about my not knowing how to run a business in India.

Finally, Diwali came around. Diwali is the festival of lights and giving. It was when I was looking to buy presents that a lightbulb went off in my head Eureka! I had to 'give' if I had to gain peace in return. The thought was simple and clear. I had to give a gift on Diwali to usher in peace in my universe or else the harassment would continue. So, I ended up giving him a gift. He then stopped harassing me and looked at me as if I was not a very bright chap. His expression was one of relief and I could almost hear his thoughts: "If only you had done this sooner, both of us could have avoided so much pain."

The whole experience had left me winded and perhaps even a bit concussed. I had started out with so many plans, but now I was beginning to understand the famous Mike Tyson quote: "Everyone has a plan until they get punched in the mouth."

Any business needs a robust plan to succeed, but be ready for punches that can throw you off your stride. Learn to roll with them and be dynamic. There was not much I could do when the mosquito inspector came into my premises. I had stood my ground but failed to absorb the punch. Nor did I learn to pivot and deflect it. Unfortunately, some of the circumstances one faces are unavoidable. It is vital that you do not let them affect your business and personal life. There can be no perfect unblemished path. There will be falls; there will be scrapes and bruises. Look at any successful entrepreneur. They are successful because they have one supernatural ability. They are able to compartmentalize these kinds of issues and do not get affected unduly by them.

Extra customization:

- If you are an entrepreneur and you are in an office or a factory, expect the local 'mosquito' inspector to visit your premises within the first few days. These guys are ruthless and smart. They are quick to spot the innocent and gullible ones. I was a strange guy in the eyes of my mosquito inspector. I would not entertain him, but I did not mind going to the court and paying fines. He would threaten me, but I was not taking the hints. He must have been flustered by my behavior. His threats would never cease. He even threatened to shut down the factory. Vandana was hysterical when she considered the potential ramifications if he carried out his threat. Tensions were running high.

- We ensured that we sent a different person every time to the court. As a fashion exporter, we had found our fashion for the courts. Our staff members would wear visibly tattered clothes. We even tailored such a 'Kurta' for the court visits. We wanted to project the image to the judge that we were poor and we ought not to be fined so often. We were hoping to reap some compassion.

- I wrote to the anti-corruption branch of Delhi Police and the CBI. I intimated to them that the concerned health and sanitary inspector wanted a bribe.

  They had bigger scalps to claim, and I received no replies. The sanitary conditions were clean. My factory was clean. But I was being harassed by the sanitary inspector. Imagine me writing to CBI complaining about the sanitary inspector. But there was no one I could complain to. The sanitary inspector is just an example of what plagues small and medium businesses in India. There are so many laws and rules in place that these inspectors take full advantage of. I am not saying that entrepreneurs in India do not do any wrong, but the majority of them are honest and have to bear the burden of the crimes committed by a very small minority. The threat to shut down our factory was real and the scary part was that it was within his powers to shut us down. Till this threat is removed, small and medium businesses across India will continue to suffer.

- The neighboring businesses did not help me. They gave me no insights into how I could deal with this issue. All they told me was that I needed to give him a 'mithai ka dabba' (box of sweets). I took it literally and went to a sweet shop. I picked up a 'barfi ka dabba.' When I gave it to him, he seemed pleased at first. He opened the box and saw that there were only barfis inside. His facial expressions were a sight to behold. Let us say that he was not pleased and left the 'dabba' behind. He wrote up a new complaint against me.

4
THE DELHI BUTTER CHICKEN

"Our world is full of people who want to tell you how to live and what to think, and they become very dangerous when anyone says no to that." — Vincent H. O'Neil

One of the inevitable aspects of running a business is receiving a multitude of opinions from all and sundry disguised as sage advice. The greatest obstacle to growth for *Saivana* came from Delhi society. Some people were keen to offer their advice and criticism without being asked. They would tell you why some things should/should not be done.

Unfortunately, I was driven by what they told me to do at times. Delhi society is a pompous and bourgeois society. It values appearances over substance. "How do you know that you are successful if you don't flaunt it. It is about faking it until you make it," they would say.

So, even if you do not have money, you have to act as if you do. You may just have Rs 100 on you, but you should portray yourself as someone who has Rs 1000 in his pocket. You are considered a loser otherwise. You are also expected to wear the trendiest clothes, be at the most happening parties, and spend lavishly.

(It is entirely another matter that those 'trendiest' clothes were probably bought in the shops of Koh Samui! ...wink) I thought of these demands as necessities. As mentioned earlier, I was influenced by what people told me. One of the first things they stressed was having the right car. If you were caught in any other contraption with four wheels, a steering wheel, and an engine, you would have committed the worst social faux pas. So, you had to buy the right car. Since *Saivana* had bagged its first few orders, I was told that I needed to be seen in the right car. What about new machines for the factory? What about upgrading the current machines? How about leasing a bigger factory?

These were the wrong questions, I was told. If I were to rephrase the lines of a popular advertisement, these things cost money, but the right car is priceless. Even my wife was pressured by her family to own the right car. "It is not right for a Delhi businessman to be seen driving a Maruti 800," was the prevalent opinion. We had to save face, and so caved in and bought a Contessa. This magnificent vehicle showed its true face only later. It was one of the biggest fuel guzzlers in the world. I think it consumed more gas in an hour than what OPEC could produce in the same time.

I admit that the car was an unproductive purchase. But we had no choice; we had to appear better than we were in reality. Anyway, these choices were not just limited to our personal lives. We were asked to abide by these rules even in the professional setting. I remember a conversation that I had with a few people. It was on a Friday evening, and as expected, I was at a party.

However, I had to leave early that day as I had a prior engagement. I informed the people I was conversing with at the party of the same. They were all surprised. They opined that the host could take it the wrong way. I, in turn, explained that I had placed an order for three machines, which were being delivered the next morning. So, my being there was necessary. However, I could hear the shocked intake of breath. All of them acted as if a small bomb had gone off. There was an eerie silence. I looked at the incredulous faces of my listeners.

After what seemed like an inordinate amount of time (it was a few seconds at most), they berated me— "What? Why? Are you stupid? Don't you know we shouldn't buy any steel or steel products on a Saturday?"

I was surprised as I was not aware of such a practice. There did not seem to be a rational reason behind it anyway. They had just stated that one should not buy steel products on a Saturday. I tried telling them that machines were a priority and we needed them up and running by Monday. The company would not deliver on a Sunday. Hence, I had to have them installed on Saturday at any cost. Dear readers, what do you think of this situation? Is it not understandable that I had no option but to receive the delivery on a Saturday?

However, these so-called friends had no sympathy toward my situation. They stressed that buying steel on Saturdays was the harbinger of doom. After passing that remark, they quickly moved away from me as if I was contagious. They were worried that they would attract 'bad karma' by simply being in my presence.

I was also advised that I could not be based out of Tughlaqabad. Why? According to them, it was a 'low-class area.' They reasoned with me that a business card with a Tughlaqabad address would be detrimental to the business. My wife Vandana was also facing pressure to move away from Tughlaqabad. All of them recommended that I shift my base to Okhla. However, Okhla would be expensive.

The lease rates would be higher, and hiring new workers would also be expensive. I was unsure about the finances involved. Would we have the money to shift? Would we be able to save money after moving? When I tried explaining my doubts to my 'well-meaning' friends, they told me that I had forgotten the most critical question. It was a simple question, but it carried enormous weight: "What would people think?" "What would people think of my business being based out of Tughlaqabad?" I was told time and again that when people thought badly of me, I would not be able to attract the right clientele and suppliers.

"What would people think?" This question was at the forefront of every decision that we had to make. We took a lot of stupid decisions driven by that question. I realized later on that the Punjabi and Delhi society did not care much about the actual situation or the ground realities. What mattered was appearances. Appearances mattered, the car you drove mattered, and the location where you stayed mattered.

If I said I stayed in South Delhi, which is where I was, it was okay. However, if I were to say that I lived in Model Town or Punjabi Bagh, I would be shunned by the South Delhi society (mind you, these are two of the affluent areas of Delhi). They considered these areas as 'low society' (LS). Readers need to be aware that when I talk about Delhi, I am talking about South Delhi in particular. I had grown up in South Delhi and Vandana also hailed from there, and we had no idea about others parts of Delhi.

So South Delhi has its own notion of what is LS and what is high society (HS). Let us take a few examples: If you lived beyond Dhaula Kuan, you were for sure LS. Noida was LS and Aurangzeb Road was a big HS. The only place that the humble people of South Delhi could not get their fix on was Gurgaon; so, to all my awesome friends staying in Gurgaon, you are hereby spared the ignominy of a tag. If you lived on the farms, it was HS. If you worked in Tughlaqabad, that was a definite LS.

Imagine major decisions about a business being driven not by business needs but by what society deems necessary. It was silly and foolish on my part to be swayed by those thoughts and assumptions. I was a greenhorn in the business world with my obvious gullibility and there was no one to help us. People judged us by our bank balance, our parents, our home, and the kind of parties we threw. Even though we were struggling, we wasted a lot of money just trying to keep up with the societal expectations and demands.

However, *Saivana*'s growth was showing an upward trend. (Perhaps, it is why we were in their good graces). I was on the constant move to land more clients. This is one of the critical steps in any enterprise: One has to keep moving.

When you are used to moving, you tend to keep moving. If you step back and rest, you will become used to that state and you will be overtaken. Do not rest on your laurels. I did not want *Saivana* to be just about that one order from Indira. The two fair visits may have seemed like expensive expeditions. However, those fairs would prove to be the long game. I had a thick address book stuffed with cards. Even though people had not placed any orders, they did leave their visiting cards. This was a different age. Today we have modern technologies like emails. The pandemic also popularized tools like Zoom and Slack. One can communicate in real-time. But back then, email communication was still in its infancy. So, it left us with one form of communication, the fax. I regularly faxed the people from whom I had taken visiting cards. People also started contacting us. We got a second order from Indira. Then we got a third order, which was bigger than the previous two.

However, Tughlaqabad came with its own set of problems. Fax only works if your telephone line works. The communication infrastructure in India was not the greatest; it was especially lacking in Tughlaqabad. I used to spend hours watching the telephone line technicians repairing the phone lines outside our factory in Tughlaqabad. I used to pay the telephone lineman to prioritize the repair of my telephone line. A missed fax was a huge catastrophe. The communications infrastructure was poor. The telephone guy became my best friend as I made sure that he received a lot of barfi boxes from time to time. Then there were the rains. We had to be careful as the drainage system too was not up to scratch in this area. The rainy season would see me devising plans to deal with flooding of the basement, which would hold up work for a number of days. I could be held up for days and weeks just trying to sort those issues out.

However, there was an unseen punch coming my way. It would spell the end of our time in Tughlaqabad. It came in the form of a Supreme Court judgment that ordered the closure of industrial units in non-industrial areas. It also directed the concerned authorities to seal and seize any units that still functioned in those areas.

I knew that we had to move quickly. The neighboring businesses scoffed at my prudence. They were so used to the Indian way of things that they could not even fathom the idea that the authorities would seal their businesses. I had no choice but to look toward Okhla. I found a factory up for lease and I signed up. It was an extremely expensive move that would significantly drain my meager financial resources. If given a choice, I would have taken some more time to find a better option.

However, time was not a luxury that was available to me. Even as I searched for an option, news filtered in of how factories in other areas were getting sealed. These news stories only served to hurry me and I was surprised by the nonchalance of my neighbors in Tughlaqabad. They were acting like the proverbial ostriches. There is a popular myth that the ostrich hides from its hunters by burying its head in the sand, the motto being 'out of sight, out of mind.' My neighbors tried to convey their concerns. They were more worried about how tense I was than they were about the sealing of their factories.

However, Vandana and I knew that we had to move out quickly. We needed some more time before the factory in Okhla would be made fit for our purpose. I was told that I needed to wait for two more months. It was a long time and I knew that we could not afford to wait that long in Tughlaqabad. I had already signed the lease and could not afford to break the contract either. I looked for a temporary, alternative solution. Fortunately, Vandana's brother, Sudhir Oberoi, graciously allowed us to move into his underground premises in South Extension. We gladly took his help and moved rapidly. It almost seemed as if we shifted everything overnight. We were gone in a trice. We were vindicated of our choice the very next week.

The authorities came into Tughlaqabad and sealed the still open factory units in the area. The authorities sealed off our factory too. However, we had moved out of those premises by then. We were now operating from Sudhir's premises. However, I would soon learn that the long arm of the law will finally catch up with you.

One and a half months later, the authorities made landfall in South Extension. They began sealing off the factory units in the area. We were caught this time and our unit too was sealed off. We were again in trouble, but this time Sudhir and his friends were able to convince the local SDM to open the seal for a couple of hours. We used the grace period to move all our garments and machines. Fortunately, the factory owner in Okhla also came through this time. He was ready to allow us to start using the premises 15 days before the agreed-upon date. Once again, in the span of one night, we had succeeded in moving our base of operations. When I look at these incidents in hindsight, I can see the divine guidance of Sai Baba and my father, who I believe looked after my family and *Saivana*. However, despite these issues, *Saivana* never failed when it came to delivering the products.

The old Indianism of "Indian garment exporters are always late" did not apply to us. We stuck to our deadlines religiously even during these tumultuous times. We never failed to deliver. We governed ourselves on one precept: our clients should not suffer. However, the Delhi society's influence also extended beyond the reaches of Delhi. It was like a python that had caught its prey. It constricted and suffocated me into making decisions that I later regretted. I remember this particular trip to Jodhpur. I was in the city to meet a few potential suppliers.

I wanted to conclude my business quickly and rush back home at the earliest. We were in the process of shipping an order, and I had to be in Delhi to ensure there were no hurdles. So, I booked a room in one of the hotels near the railway station.

I had got a great price, and I could catch the train quickly. However, trouble brewed when my business associates could not find me at a party where I was on the invite list; so, they called me to find out where I was. I informed them that I was in Jodhpur on some business.

When they heard that I was in Jodhpur, they inquired about Umaid Bhawan. They asked if I found the hotel as good as advertised. I tried to explain that I was staying at a different hotel.

They expressed their disappointment that I did not choose to stay at 'the 5-star hotel' in the city, which was Umaid Bhawan. Thirty minutes later, I received a call from another well-wisher. He spent some time trying to convince me that it was imperative for me to stay at Umaid Bhawan. It would convey an important message to everybody that I could afford to stay in such a hotel.

All my justifications melted away in the face of that magic question. It did not matter how logical my decision and actions were. Imagine playing rock-paper-scissors. You could throw up scissors hoping that your opponent chooses the palm and shows paper. However, what if he instead throws you a sign that says what would people think if you beat them. It may be an exaggerated example. But this question, "What would people think?", transcends all boundaries and changes the game completely. There is no sense and logic.

That question has to trump any reason. Thus, I changed hotels and moved to Umaid Bhawan. Could I afford the change? Was there any financial prudence in my move? Did it make the negotiations any easier? The answer to all these questions is a big resounding NO. However, there was one change. I was late getting to the railway station and almost missed my train.

I had to move to a luxurious hotel even though I could not afford it. We were living outside our means. This was foolishness 101. How foolish can you be if your business and personal decisions are driven by what other people think? I was also persuaded into investing in certain projects. If you are a budding entrepreneur, you will be advised to invest in sure-fire investments. I was also beguiled into several such schemes.

We followed the trend and invested our already depleted and meager savings into certain projects. We invested in some real estate projects, but they never took off. We made stupid financial decisions, not based on logic or research but simply on the word of others. These were fair-weather friends. There is this famous joke: Success is relative—the more successful you are, the more people will come forward claiming to be your relatives.

So, the moment there is a whiff of failure, you will find yourself struck off the party list invites. Then you are struck by FOMO when you are not invited to a certain wedding. I thank God there was no Facebook or anything else like it in those days! Missing these events only exacerbates your low self-esteem. Well, we invested in a few hare-brained schemes even when we felt it was not the wise thing to do as a lack of investment meant a lack of funds. We hoped our investments would yield good dividends to build up our resources.

Such thoughtless expenditure just for keeping up appearances is likely to result in your suddenly running perilously short of money. The Contessa had unmasked itself finally. It ran up huge gas bills. But hey! It was a Contessa, after all. How about any other reasonable car? Of course not! That would be terribly low class!

I have another funny story about the Contessa. When I first bought the car, Delhi society insisted that the Contessa had to be taken to the temple to be blessed. I had to get it blessed so that the car would not be in an accident. Accidents were not an indictment of one's lack of driving skills. They were an indictment of the lack of divine blessings. So, my wife and I went to the temple in the car. I remember that the road to the temple was a bit steep and narrow. However, I was able to drive the car into the temple without any incident. The puja was carried out and the car was blessed. Then I had to back out of the temple.

There was no scope to make a turn. I had to drive out of the temple in reverse gear. I took my time as the car was new and I did not want to be in an accident. It took me five minutes to completely back out of the road and reach the main motorway. My neck was stiff from constantly looking back to avoid any potential accident. It went flawlessly. I let out a sigh of relief and rolled my stiff neck around in order to relax it. Suddenly, we heard a loud thud. We looked back in shock and found that a cyclist had crashed into the car. There was a huge scratch on the car. My wife was horrified and berated me for my driving. I can tell you with great confidence that I am a great driver. After that day, I have never taken a car to the temple.

Coincidentally, my cars have never been in an accident either, touch wood! The Contessa, in a couple of years, needed to be upgraded. The flavor of the month then was the Daewoo. We had leveraged ourselves to the extreme at the very early stages of our business.

This is the case with success. Even as you gain friends, you also make enemies without even realizing it. Success attracts envy. Failure attracts contempt as you are discarded from the invitation lists.

I remember hosting a party on the terrace of my house with my limited means. The party was panned universally—terrible food and terrible decorations. Well, they praised my party to the high heavens as a great party to my face, but they whispered behind my back and mocked my efforts. The garage was still being used as a stockroom for some fabrics. People sniffed at the sight. Those people never turned up at my parties again. I was never invited to their parties either.

Delhi society has had a huge influence on *Saivana*'s growth and missteps. If I had focused on the core growth of my business instead of catering to the whims and fancies of Delhi society, I could have done much better. This is a trend in North Indian and Punjabi families.

There is a reason why there are not many Punjabis among the richest families in India. Most of them are too busy being opulent rather than consolidating and growing their wealth. The whiskey has to keep flowing and the Chicken Tikka and Chola Bhatura have to be constantly replenished and never run out. It is just a party, and you need to dress the part.

However, thankfully, I stood firm on one aspect. I had no access to banking accounts and bank managers. The Delhi parties would mean that you could meet such people. Entrepreneurship was still a novel concept, and start-ups would become a part of the commercial lexicon in a few years in the next millennium. Back then, you needed a good relationship with bank managers to extend your credit limits. However, Delhi society also demands you only do your banking with certain banks.

I was doing my transactions with a nationalized bank. I received a lot of heat for not banking with an MNC. It did not matter if I had built a rapport with the bank staff. People kept exhorting the benefits of doing business with an MNC. Luckily, I never succumbed to that pressure. I stuck with a nationalized bank that was based out of Chennai. Later it would be amalgamated into the Indian Overseas Bank. The bank managers helped me grow. They had a huge hand in *Saivana*'s growth. They extended lines of credit based on my word. I had no collateral. But they trusted me and opened lines of credit. I used to joke with them that they could keep me as collateral. If payments were not made, I would stay in the bank. Or I would even give them the keys to my Contessa. The one good thing was that the Contessa was still considered a status symbol. Thus, the car was the only reliable asset I held.

But my bank managers trusted me. Local bank managers at that time had greater autonomy and did not need to run everything by their Regional Office or Head Office. My bank managers were young and dynamic and were from Chennai. They enjoyed great freedom in making decisions, and they trusted me, and I am happy to say that I repaid their trust. Local bank managers do not enjoy the same autonomy these days.

I do not know whether *Saivana* would have scaled the same level of success under the banking conditions of today. However, I understand the need to limit their authority due to the number of scams that plagued Indian banking in those years.

Saivana only grew with time. Our reputation for adherence to deadlines and quality control started to percolate to other potential clients. The word was out: *Saivana* was a trustworthy partner. We did not need any other advertisement. Word of mouth found us great clients. One such client was Isabel Marant. She was a young fashion designer and had just started her career when she reached out to us. She was looking for a firm just like *Saivana*. The goodwill and reputation that we had built ensured that she too heard of our reliability. She found us and contacted us. We knew within the first few conversations that we had come across a genius.

We knew that this was a deal we had to land. So, we made a few trips to Paris to meet her. We have built a great professional and personal friendship with her over the years. She is one of the biggest designers in Paris today. We have had this association since 1998. We piggybacked on her success and growth. Today she is family to us and we are greatly indebted to her.

It was a testament to her and the people who worked with her, in particular Virginie Croisier, who stood by *Saivana* through thick and thin. It has now been a good many years and it is a testament to Isabel's skills that she has grown so much in the fashion world and her key people, such as Virginie and Marie, have remained with her (and us). It would really not have been possible without them.

Another great client we gained was Bonpoint, the children's iconic fashion label. Its founder Marie-France became a great friend of ours and encouraged us to grow with the brand. At first, I laughed when we got the first order for baby garments. I think their first order was for 100-odd pieces. Eventually and over time, their order size reached 100,000 pieces per year. We do not work with them anymore but we have many fond memories of working with Marie-France.

She still calls us from time to time to start on a new project in Africa and God bless her, even at this age, she has not lost her entrepreneurial zest. In fact, it was due to her we became the primary suppliers to her start-up store called Merci which in French means 'Thank You.' Merci changed the way of shopping in Paris as it also had a great coffee shop attached to it (or rather the garment shop was within the coffee shop). Most proceeds from Merci were earmarked for charity and it gave us great satisfaction to be a part of such a project. The fact that Vandana had been one of the best students in her class came in handy when one of her professors introduced us to a buyer from Denmark called Jan Machenhauer. Jan's patterns were so perfect that Vandana could further her learning in the field of pattern making. Jan had a small shop in Copenhagen and it gave us an opportunity to explore the Danish market in the formative years of *Saivana*.

We loved Copenhagen and while visiting there, we came across an awesome person by the name of Susanne Rutzou. She went on to become one of the topmost Danish designers and we have such fond memories of her. It was a real pleasure working with her. Copenhagen still remains one of my favorite cities in the world.

Another of our new buyers was Guy Perdon from Paris. He and his lovely wife Marie-France had a small brand and Guy was a big fan of India. With a sweater always wrapped around his neck and chain-smoking, Guy was the quintessential French man. He gave us a lot of support and orders and that helped *Saivana* tremendously. Guy and his wife became good friends with us and even after they closed their brand, we still remained in touch. His house outside of Paris was just superb and we had some good French wine and food there.

Another bad influence of Delhi society was to scoff at the idea of savings. More money could be made via investment in stocks and shares. I considered myself a smart economist, and I thought, why not?

At every party, I would hear people brag about the money they made. This was the age of Harshad Mehta and Ketan Parekh. So once more, my focus was diverted away from my core business. I spent every morning at my share broker's office. I would sit in front of a computer and trade in shares.

I was making some good returns, and I was emboldened to put in more money. The first three years after starting *Saivana*, I put all our savings into the stock market based on fantastical stories. I was swayed by the reports of easy money.

There were innumerable tips: Buy shares of XYZ or ABC. They all told of the prospects of each of these companies and how money could be made hand over fist. They used to tell me, "Sikka! Guaranteed the prices will go up! Guaranteed you will get 10 times returns."

So, I was hooked on buying more shares. However, it all came tumbling down after the Big Fat Bulls went bust. Our share broker made lots of money due to insider trading and fled the country.

The best part was that the share broker was actually my childhood friend from school and there had not been one whiff from him on what shares would go up or crash. Meanwhile, on the sidelines, he was building his own portfolio based on inside information; and then one day, when it was all over, he fled the country. It has been over 25 years now, but to date, I have not heard a 'Hello' or a 'Hi' from him. That experience left a bitter taste in my mouth.

Eventually, the price of the shares that I had with me was not even worth the price of the paper it was printed on; it was not even worth the price of toilet paper. Shares then were printed on physical paper and not traded digitally. I had diverted our precious financial resources into foolish endeavors influenced by the Delhi Butter Chicken gang. If there is something I have to stress based on my experiences, it is this: There are bound to be distractions. Do not lose focus on your core business.

If there is one thing that you can learn from my experience, it is that you do not have to act on every piece of advice that people give you. It is essential that you remember this because people are sure to give you unsolicited advice. However, it is you who has to live through the consequences and not them. If people provide you with advice, keep an open mind. Consider their advice to broaden your perspective.

Philip E. Tetlock once said that great decision makers are like foxes. They are nimble, flexible, and adaptable. So, when someone gives their advice, do not think of it as the only answer. Do not interpret the world with just one big idea. Use their inputs to look at the world through a different lens. If people provide you with more advice, look at the world through each of those perspectives. Weigh the consequences of each choice. When you weigh the consequences, it would be for the best if you think in terms of probabilities and not absolutes. Look beyond the shades of black and white as life can be more complicated than just two polar scenarios. So, when you receive a piece of advice, use it to broaden your perspective.

Think of the possible consequences and how they could affect you. Move only when you are comfortable with the consequences. If you are not okay, then reconsider the advice given.

"Keep away from people who try to belittle your ambitions. Small people always do that, but the really great make you feel that you, too, can become great."

- Mark Twain

5
CHICKEN LABORDOR

"The dignity of labor depends not on what you do, but how you do it." —
Edwin Osgood Grover

A happy worker is a productive worker. This was one of the key takeaways from my MBA. I was taught to see workers as assets and always keep them close. I had also read books on how successful business leaders were close to their workforce and how that closeness contributed to their success. I was determined to follow their example. When we moved to Tughlaqabad, we slowly scaled up, and our labor force also grew. At one point, we had around 40 people on our payroll.

I was very close to the staff. I showed no discrimination. I sat with them during lunch hours, and we shared our packed lunches. I had fostered a communal atmosphere where we felt like a family. On the occasions when we had to work late into the night, I would drive down to Moolchand, a place famed for its egg parathas, and get some parathas packed along with tea for our employees.

I ensured that I always conveyed my appreciation for the work they did. Despite this closeness, there were some problematic elements within the workforce.

They had joined a labor union with all the 40 employees on board. I had no clue about these developments. I was inexperienced, and I was not aware that the labor laws in India were chaotic at that juncture. They caught on to my lack of experience. I had no proper documentation concerning my employees. I had no written contracts of any nature that established our working relationship. People often came to me looking for a job, and if there was a position vacant, I would test their qualifications and capabilities. If they fulfilled all the requirements, I offered them the job.

I relied on one person to be my right-hand man. He was my go-to person for any discussion about the workforce. We had built an easy rapport and even considered each other as friends. He helped me assess any potential new hire. I had given him a free reign to manage the workforce to ensure that we met our deadlines. I saw his appointment as a motivating measure to the workers. If they would work well, they too would be given additional responsibilities. I wanted to impress on them that the workplace could be a home. According to the legal documents, the company may have been owned by Vandana, but I wanted the employees to understand that their contribution was always valued. We instituted many practices within the company to drive this idea. I shall cover some of these practices later in this chapter.

I also relied on my secretary for the paperwork. She looked after the documentation work in the company. Unbeknownst to me, my right-hand man started a romantic relationship with her. She leaked the company's financial and order details to her paramour. They were thick as thieves, and this issue reared its venomous head at one of the most critical times in the infancy of *Saivana*.

It all began when I came across two of my employees napping in the factory during work hours. I could not tolerate such a lax attitude. I had spoken to all my employees about honesty and integrity in their work. I was paying them generously, and I wanted them to be honest. I knew it would set a bad precedent if I overlooked their actions. So, I immediately fired them. I wanted the workplace to hold integrity and discipline.

I expected that my quick action would send the signal that such behavior would not be tolerated. I wanted the incident to serve as a deterrent. However, it was then that I realized that the workers had joined a labor union. So, when I fired the two people, all hell broke loose. The workers came running down the steps to my office. I could sense their anger by the din of their footsteps. Their angry screams reached me before they arrived at my door. They banged at the door, and it gave way to their rage. I could see it in their faces. They wanted to beat me up. Their thirst for violence was palpable.

I tried to pacify the angry mob. I asked them, "What happened?" They asked me, "How could you fire those two people? How could you dare to do such an action?" Their threatening voices only gained decibels with every word. They threatened to beat me, and I was shaking in my boots. One of the workers was holding a pair of scissors. He imitated the action of stabbing me. The blade kissed the edge of my shirt button near my midriff. He paused. It happened so quickly that I could not even move back in reflex. I was petrified with fear.

Even as the sweat collected on my brow, I told them as calmly as possible, "You may beat me today to vent this anger. But what will you do tomorrow when the law hunts you down with no mercy?" The man tapped my button as if to elevate the tension. Then he withdrew his hand. I foolishly thought that he had seen reason.

But then he told me, "We won't work today." He turned to the people behind him and said, "Shut down the factory. He has a car, right? Let us burn it to a crisp and send him a much-needed message." He had whipped up the crowd that was massed behind him. He then led them outside, threatening violence and arson. I was helpless as the era of mobile phones was still a few years away, and the only line of communication was the landline telephones.

I was still standing trying to gather my wits. I could feel the adrenaline pumping in my body as I stood contemplating my near death. It was at this time that my tired brain recollected that the man who almost stabbed me was the one who I considered as my right-hand man.

He was the one who was now threatening to burn down my car. The crowd went outside the factory, and I could see that some red flags had been unfurled.

To this day, I wonder where those flags had been stacked away as I had never seen them on the factory premises previously. I could hear the loud cries of someone asking for kerosene to burn my car. *"Kerosene lao. Iski car jalao."* These cries reverberated through the air.

As I mentioned in the previous chapter, the Contessa was the only asset I owned. The car was parked at the end of the by-road as it could not enter the road that led up to my factory. That road was the only way in or out. The mob then shouted slogans and blocked the road. They shouted their threats that they were going to keep me locked in and not allow me to leave.

The unorganized sector in India features factories like the one I was in at this moment. There was no clear demarcated area for industries. Small and medium-sized enterprises like mine operated out of such small factories in suburban areas. Thus, I was stuck in my office with no respite. My first call of distress was to the helpline number, 100, to call the cops. But I did not receive any help from that end as the number seemed to be out of use. Luckily, I remembered that I had the number of a person who was the President of the student body of a nearby college. He wielded considerable influence in this area. I had made his acquaintance a while back. I remembered my conversation with him. He had said, "Rajat Bhai, if you ever encounter a problem, just give me a call."

So, I called him. I was panicking, and I told him, "Bhai! Please come quickly. These people have locked me up and are going to burn my car. I am sure that they will kill me." He assured me that he would be there at the earliest. I looked out the window and saw my workers scream, "Rajat Sikka Murdabad!"

I could see their faces, and I remembered the lunches and dinners I had shared with them. I could remember the camaraderie we had built as we talked about our families. I remembered the Diwali pujas we had taken part in together as a company. I remembered the gifts I had given them on special occasions.

The faces that I now saw had no resemblance to the joyful and smiling faces in my memory. They were snarling and hurling insults at me.

A Maruti 800 rolled into the street within 10 minutes of my call. It was a scene straight out of a common commercial Bollywood film. Four six-foot men stepped out of the car. They were all armed with hockey sticks. They looked at the crowd of 40 or so people. They slowly took a step toward them. I could see the crowd collectively take a step back. The four men charged at them after what seemed a long second. The crowd immediately scampered away in fright from the four men who were at their back screaming their curses. Thus, I was rescued from my factory.

Then like they do in every lame Indian joke, the police finally turned up. They did a lockout. It meant that no one would be allowed into the premises. I could see the end of *Saivana* flash in front of my eyes. I knew that a lockout would be the death knell for my fledgling business. I had no workforce, the garments that had to be shipped were within the premises, and I could not enter the factory anymore. I went home that night, shaken to my core. An urgent shipment had to go out and all the cuttings for the garments were inside the premises.

Somehow, we got the cuttings out of there but we had no place to work from. This is where my good friend Mohit Soni (Rahul) came to the rescue. He had a spare room available in his house in Greater Kailash-1 and we could use that as our office premises. I still remember Vandana trying to sort out the cutting in that room, one piece at a time (the order was for 700 odd pieces). She sorted out the cutting and we gave it to a fabricator to do the stitching and finishing, while I sorted out the labor crisis. Frankly speaking, I had no clue as to what I had to do next. Sudhir again came to my rescue; he introduced me to his friend Lucky Wadhawan, who in turn introduced me to his labor consultant in Okhla (Lucky was running his own units in Okhla and was well conversant with the labor laws). That person assured me that he would arrange a meeting with the Deputy Labor Commissioner to help sort the dispute.

I needed urgent help as the lockout was set for a duration of 15 days. The Deputy Labor Commissioner understood my problems and asked me if I wanted to continue with the same workforce. I said, "No." These people wanted to kill me. There was no chance I wanted to work with them again. Then he told me that the only way to get out of this mess was to pay them off to leave. He knew that I had no knowledge of the labor laws and helped me. The negotiations were tense.

However, I wanted them out of my life as quickly as possible, and every day that my factory was in a lockout, I stood to lose more. It was now that the information that they had gotten from my secretary came into play. They held all the aces. They knew the financial and order details and dragged the negotiations to seize the best possible payout. So, they pushed the days and demanded exorbitant amounts, and we came to an agreement after much haggling. The amounts were still astronomical.

My former right-hand man secured himself a deal of Rs 70,000 (an astonishing amount, considering this was in 1996). When it was time for me to make the payouts, I insisted on two conditions. First, the payment would be made within the premises of my bank. Second, I wanted my bank manager to be the one to make the payments. The reasons were twofold.

One, I did not want to see them again. Two, I wanted to avoid a scenario where they could come back later and say that I had forced them to accept unfair payouts by threatening them. Once again, my bank manager came to my rescue. He assured me that he would take care of it and guaranteed that his staff would work beyond the 4 p.m. closing time of the bank to complete the transactions in a day. My former staff members came in on their own time, collected the payments, and left.

When I stepped into my factory 15 days later, I was a bit broken. All that I had accomplished in the past eight months had gone down the drain. I had to start all over again. I had no choice but to pick myself up. I sent faxes to all my buyers in Paris asking for an extension of the delivery dates.

I apologized and informed them that the circumstances were out of my control. But I took responsibility for the delay. I also offered them a discount of 30 percent. I informed them that while they did not ask for a discount, I offered them the discount as proof of my good faith and intentions. I also told them that there would be no further delays in the orders.

When I had to start all over again, I was quick to recognize my deficiencies. I hired a labor consultant who drew up the contracts; he was to do so for all my future hires as well. He then advised me, "Rajat, I don't want you to be interacting with the labor force on a daily basis. Hire an HR executive to deal with the labor. Your temperament is different, and you have been educated abroad. What you learned abroad will not help you deal with the ground realities in India. If you start interacting with your employees daily, you will be embroiled in one labor dispute after another. When you are stuck with this logjam, you will no longer be able to focus on your business."

I took him up on his advice and used the contracts drafted by him to hire afresh for all the vacant roles in the company. I also hired an HR manager as advised. This hire was one of the trickiest decisions for *Saivana* even today. I shall discuss this thorny issue later in this chapter. However, over the years and even today, I have had labor disputes. They are unavoidable, and if you are an entrepreneur, you should make yourself aware of the labor laws. Do not be slack on that count. Even big Indian companies like Maruti have seen violent labor disputes. So, be aware and vigilant even if you think of yourself as the most generous boss.

Although I have faced labor disputes, I must stress that Indian workers are very hard-working. They are diligent and work to the best of their capacities. Perhaps it is the goodness and integrity of the vast majority of workers that has ensured that my faith in the Indian workers still remains. I still subscribe to the idea that a happy worker is a productive worker. But I am far more vigilant and careful today. However, the diligence of the workforce comes to a standstill during festivals.

Many of my migrant workers want to travel back home during the holidays. I have always maintained that *Saivana* did not solely belong to Rajat and Vandana. I gave many inspiring talks of how it also belonged to them. However, when it came to festivals like Diwali and Eid, these speeches would fall on deaf ears. They insisted on going home.

I do not blame them for their decision to go home. It is one of the ground realities in India that most of the labor is migratory. I empathized with their need to be with their families on such momentous occasions. So, we set up a calendar. Every December, we would look at the next year's calendar to identify these key holidays. We knew that there would be serious disruption in work around those dates. So, we assigned those days as holidays and planned our work schedule around them.

When I speak of holidays, I cannot help but reference the lies told by many workers. I remember one particular incident. One day, a man walked up to me and told me with tears in his eyes that his mother had passed away. He wanted to go home for the last rites. I did not tarry.

I immediately pulled out some cash from my wallet to finance his ticket home and gave him compassionate leave. About 15 or 16 months later, the same man walked into my office. His face was grave, and I knew that something was wrong. He broke down into tears once more and told me that his mother had passed away and he had to go home for the last rites!

I was taken aback. I asked him, "How is it possible? Didn't your mother pass away last year?" He stuttered and realized that he had forgotten that he had offered the same reason for obtaining leave the previous year.

Suddenly, he came back with the response that it was his stepmother. I was apprehensive, but I did not want to be overly suspicious. I gave him some money for the train ride home and approved his leave. Two years later, he told me that his brother had passed away. He asked for leave again the next year, stating that another brother had passed away.

Many such people came to me citing many such unfortunate mishaps. I helped all of them with some money to travel as I knew the importance of family. But many people forgot the person they said had passed away and came back with the same reason a year or two down the line. It may seem like I am painting these blue-collar workers in a negative light. However, in my experience, even white-collar workers can spin some fantastic yarns.

They can start lying right from the moment you first cross paths. I have seen innumerable resumes where I can identify the exaggerations. They portray themselves as perfectionists. They will act as if they are the salve for all the problems. In practice, they end up becoming the biggest problem. I have seen many interviews where people would strut in and talk a good game.

However, they fail miserably when they are asked to walk the talk. I remember one interview where I was hiring for a sales associate. In his CV, the candidate had written that he could speak three languages: English, Hindi, and French.

I was delighted, and as soon as he walked in, I started, "Bonjour. Comment Allez-Vous?" It meant, "Hello. How do you do?" He was stumped, and only one sound escaped his mouth, "Huh?" I repeated my French greeting. He had no reply.

I laughed and told him, "Boy, do not lie on your CV. You will be found out. You may get the job by exaggerating your skills, but it is the actual strength of your skills that will help you keep your job." I had no choice but to nix his interview immediately.

There were other commonalities that I started noticing in interviews. One of the questions I used to ask candidates was the reason why they quit their previous jobs. I used to receive two responses far more commonly than any other. One was that they wanted to grow, and the second was that their previous company was going bankrupt. However, when we looked into the background of these candidates, many of those who claimed to be looking for growth had actually been let go from their roles. In the latter case, we found that the company was doing well, but the concerned person was a poor worker.

When we came across many such cases, we standardized the practice of running background checks on all our potential new hires. After having hired and fired many employees, I have a piece of advice for any aspiring entrepreneur. If you are planning to hire a new employee, you should not forget to ask one critical question during the interview. **What is your biggest failure?** Ask that question in all your interviews. Then ask them how they coped with their failure. What was the emotional, mental, and physical blowback from the said failure? How did they manage those blowbacks? Ask them these questions.

If you come across a candidate who says they have never failed in their career, end the interview quickly. You need not consider such a candidate. Why? Because people will fail at one point or the other. There is no shame in that. Even in my story, you can see the number of failures I faced. You should be looking to hire people who can respond to such setbacks better than the rest. You are not looking for the perfect candidate. You are looking for a candidate with the perfect response to failure.

One of the key issues you have to note as a manufacturing entrepreneur is the formation of unions within your premises. Indian labor unions can be the death knell for any entrepreneur. I would like to note that I do not oppose trade unions. When I studied abroad, I was a hardcore socialist. However, my experiences with Indian labor unions have shifted my perspective. Their behavior and interactions transformed me into a capitalist. I have been fair to my employees. I have never underpaid them and have always treated them very well. However, a minor issue is enough reason for trade unions to declare a strike.

If you take a car around the Delhi suburbs, you will find one peculiar but common sight. Observe the tea shops—there will be one person sitting beside a blackboard. The board will say that it is a garment worker trade union. It will also state that the union has been recognized by the Indian government. This person will preside over the happenings and incidents in factories and determine the action to be taken.

Those tea shops serve as command centers for trade unions. My dislike for the unions comes from these leaders. They are corrupt and are only looking to fatten their wallets. There have been occasions when I had to negotiate with such leaders. They will hint that they can be bought off. They hold these dharnas and protests in the name of employee welfare but come to the negotiating table looking for a piece of the pie instead. I have tried to tell my employees innumerable times that their first call for any grievance has to be the HR office and not the union. I tried explaining that we could resolve their issues faster than the union would. Over the years, I have taken a hard-line stance toward the unions. Whenever they presented unreasonable demands, I have not hesitated in going to the courts to find the resolution.

I have also found trouble with office romances. I am a big believer in love and have no reservations about it. Come on, I have seen DDLJ at least 50 times by now! But I have come across office affairs that have been detrimental to *Saivana*'s growth. There was the case of my former secretary and one of the workers on the floor. Then I also encountered another situation where one of the senior merchandising managers was having an extramarital affair with a man who was a cutting master. The problem arose when I discovered that the manager was covering for her paramour's mistakes, and the man covered up the mistakes of the manager. I am an old-fashioned romantic, but how do I deal with these issues?

No MBA degree will prepare you for these issues. I have to mention that these love affairs were well-documented and not based on hearsay. Whenever I called the woman to the office to highlight some issues, her paramour also entered with her to protect her. I had to let go of both of them. This was not a unique case. I had to fire many senior managers who masked the errors of their partners.

However, I drew the line when it came to matters of sexual harassment. I had no tolerance for any kind of sexual harassment. *Saivana* was owned by a woman. We wanted the staff to know that women would have a safe space within our premises. I even fired two men who engaged in what is known as loose locker room talk.

There was no space for innuendos or double entendres that impinged the modesty of women. From the inception of *Saivana*, we had a policy that women would not work overtime. They had to leave the premises by 6 p.m.

In the early days, when there was no proper public transport infrastructure available near my factory, I personally drove these women in my car to the nearby bus stand so that they could reach home safely. It is a policy that we follow to this day that women are not allowed to work past 6 p.m.

I am extremely proud to say that *Saivana* has followed many hallmark policies from its very inception. One of them has to do with hiring. We have never discriminated against anyone. The last name, caste, religion, gender, or sexuality—none of these were even a topic of discussion.

All we cared about was the candidate's capability. Can the person fulfill the role assigned to her/him? If the answer was yes, they were hired. We have built a name for being fair and just in our hiring standards, and we intend on living up to it. I am also proud of how we have never missed a single salary payment. On the seventh of every month, our employees would receive their salaries. Unfailingly. Even in our lean times, I ensured that my employees were paid on time. If I had to beg and borrow from different quarters, I did not mind. My employees had to receive their salaries on the seventh. That check on the seventh of every month meant they had a secure job, because job insecurity can be a killer. That check paid for the food in their homes, the education of their children, the care of their elderly parents, and so on.

A lot of Indian entrepreneurs claim to hate salary day and I wonder why. Whenever salary day comes along, I always thank Sai Baba that we have the money to pay all our people; moreover, they have worked hard and earned it. Salary day should be a day of celebration, just like these days, a haircut for me is a celebration of life (you get the idea). It means the organization is strong and moving ahead and its people are always prospering. As we grew, I have had the pleasure of working with many stellar people.

They were honest and had integrity. Some of them have been with me from the beginning. However, one has to deal with the other extreme as well. At every stage, I have had people who joined the company simply to incite chaos. They would look to whip up the workers to go on strikes against the management.

However, the biggest problem I have faced as a garment businessman is the tobacco addiction of workers. My workers bought the Gutkha pouches in bulk and chewed tobacco regularly. My primary concern was not just about their health. They are adults and have the freedom to make their choices in life. I was more worried about the stains they would leave on the fabric when the workers spat it out. Scientists are yet to discover or invent a detergent that can wash away the orange stains of betel quid. Even a single stain can cause the garment to be labeled as damaged and discarded.

We tried several steps to combat this issue. One step was to inspect the belongings of the workers as they entered the factory. When workers realized that they could not carry the chewing tobacco inside, they became creative. They stuffed the pouches in their underwear and socks. The security guard could not check those areas. Once they were inside, they would go to the bathrooms when they felt the urge to chew. They would consume it in the bathrooms and come back to their workspace. If they were caught chewing, they would offer the excuse that they had gone out and bought a packet. It is not appropriate to put cameras in the restrooms either. It is an issue that we contend with to date.

I also discovered one of the most unique facets of Indian migrant labor: the committee. While the name may seem familiar, it served a different purpose entirely. The committee would consist of 10 to 12 people. Every month they would contribute Rs 100 to the group. They would then use this collection whenever there was an emergency or a function.

If one of the committee members was getting his daughter married, he would use the entire collection to fund the function. If there was a medical emergency for any of the committee members, the collection would be used.

One person would take the entire sum collected at the end of the eleventh month if there were no such events. Then they would resume the committee collection once more from scratch. The person who would get the final lump sum was decided based on turns. The migrant laborers generally followed this practice. They never felt the pinch as they were only giving Rs 100 every month, and they received a huge lump sum at the end if it was their turn. It sounds ideal in theory.

In reality, there could be several issues. These committee collections are kept by one person in the committee and not deposited in banks. The committees are mistrustful of the banks, and they are the backbone of the labor market in India. The problem arises if the person entrusted with the responsibility runs away with the money. I have faced this issue several times. It is not easy to catch such runaways. They simply disappear into the mass migrant labor market.

I have had to battle the prejudices of our employees as well. I remember one of my early conversations with a worker. We talked about his family, and he told me how he was managing to send his sons to school. I remembered that he also had two daughters. I asked him about their education, and he seemed to think it was unnecessary.

My liberal upbringing could not accept such a blind spot. My wife and I agreed that we had to step in to do something immediately. We instituted a policy where we told our workers that if they produced the monthly bills for their daughters' education, we would pay them the amount. It could be her school fees, uniform fees, money for textbooks, etc.

If they produced the bills, we would reimburse the payment. My wife was the soul of *Saivana*'s operations, and we wanted more girls to be able to achieve the same.

However, we had to discontinue that policy for a while when we discovered a few tricks being played. One of the workers came to us with a bill that said Rs 1650. It was obvious that the number 1 was added by the worker. The bill should have been for Rs 650.

However, when we dug a little deeper, we discovered the true nastiness of the worker. He did not have children, and he was faking the bills to pocket the money himself.

Today, we have resumed the policy once more, but we are far more stringent now. Internal corruption is a huge problem in all companies. I just mentioned the example of how one person faked the bills to pocket extra money. I have fired people in the purchasing department for producing fake bills. I remember one person fainting in fear when I summoned him to my office to question some of his submitted bills.

I have come across various schemes used by workers and even the management to make some extra money on the side. In isolation, some of the schemes were excellent, and I can even admire them for their ingenuity. However, in the cold light of day, these schemes came at the expense of *Saivana*, and I can never forgive or forget such acts.

I have faced the brunt of internal corruption. There have been people who would purchase supplies and tack on extra amounts to the bill to pocket the difference. This corruption has not been limited to blue-collar workers. I have seen even white-collar workers lured by the prospect of making some extra cash on the side. There have been instances where people from the accounts department delayed payments to suppliers. They would only carry out the payment if the supplier gave a cut to the concerned person. I have not tolerated such crooks in my company.

If they were caught, they would be fired without hesitation. I then instituted a policy that no supplier could wait more than 20 minutes to be paid. If they had to wait more than that allotted time, everyone in the accounts department would be docked one day's pay. In all my years at *Saivana*, I have never worried about external competition. I have always worried about internal corruption.

Two departments have seen the greatest employee attrition rates at our firm. One is the Fabric Purchasing Department and the other is Human Resources. The corruption in purchasing fabrics can be checked.

If a staff member submitted a bill saying that he or she purchased cotton at the rate of Rs 35 per kilogram, I could cross-check. If I suspected that the supplier had an agreement with my employee, I would call another supplier to inquire about the rate of cotton.

If he quotes me a rate of Rs 32 per kilogram, I would have questions for my employee. I have also had to deal with employees stealing goods from the factory. They would steal clothes that were cut or discarded and sell them to someone else. They would steal other bits and bobs to sell. Scissors were a particular favorite. However, it is white-collar corruption that can trap you. You would not know it until it hits you. Earlier in the chapter, I mentioned how I had to hire an HR professional. In over 25 years of *Saivana*'s existence, I have had over 15 to 17 HR managers. I have caught many of them stealing money. Some of them hired people they knew and took a cut from their salary payments.

One of the most shocking discoveries I made was that the drivers we hired were not cleaning the vehicles. They were hired with the understanding that they would also be the ones cleaning and maintaining the vehicles. So, imagine my surprise when I found that they had successfully persuaded the HR department to hire helpers to do these tasks.

I immediately conducted an audit and found 85 people in redundant roles. The helpers had hired other helpers. Many of these helpers came from the same village and had a connection to the HR staff. The HR members could rely on that connection to take a cut out of their salaries for themselves. I have also been subject to such blatant nepotism by HR managers. They would want to hire people they knew and could influence quickly. There have been occasions where the HR manager would tell me of the problems of a particular employee. It could be that the person is a thief or that he or she is a poor worker. When the HR manager warns me of a particular employee, I have no choice but to take heed.

If they recommended a firing, I accepted it as I had to trust them to do their job. But there have been occasions when I found that certain people were targeted due to internal politics.

I have also faced issues with HR managers who could only deal with the grievances of the management; they would be utterly hapless when it came to dealing with the grievances of the workers. Then there were a couple of managers who were talented in dealing with the workers but failed miserably to deal with the management.

If there is one appointment you should get right, it is the appointment of a competent HR manager. I cannot stress this point enough. I have come to realize the importance of the role due to the high turnover at this post in *Saivana*. Most people have the wrong idea about HR managers. They think that the role of the HR manager is to hire staff and ensure that they are paid on time and keep track of employee performance metrics, etc. But these duties are almost clerical in nature. These are the roles of a personnel manager rather than an HR manager. The gambit of an HR manager is far more diverse. They have to be adept at spotting weaknesses in current employees. Then they should be able to identify how those weaknesses can be addressed. Would a training course help? Do they need to assign a coach or mentor?

Isaac Asimov, the famous science fiction writer, once wrote, "Violence is the last refuge of the incompetent." If I could modify the quote, sackings are the last resort of incompetent HR managers. HR managers should not look at employees as numbers on a tracking sheet. They have to be human and understand their failings and help them address those failings. They need to be able to develop robust training programs. Perhaps the performance metrics are the problem. They need to design a better system. Such skilled HR managers are a rare find.

The entrepreneurs among the readers may now have a valid question: How do you deal with internal corruption? Do you have to micromanage every process? I would recommend that you have a firm grasp of the operations. However, do not be too involved in your company's operations; I shall address this particular point in a later chapter. What you could do is build a robust financial system and have multiple points of checks and balances to verify the transactions. Conduct surprise checks to keep people on their toes.

Have a zero-tolerance policy. If you find someone corrupt, do not hesitate to fire that person. Such prompt action can serve as a deterrent.

If I could provide one final tip, you cannot totally stop internal corruption. There will be a leak somewhere. Much like how water seeps into any well-built building, there will always be places from where some funds could be siphoned off. Do not let them dictate your mind. Strengthen your systems and be vigilant; rectify the loopholes as and when you find them.

If you want to be an entrepreneur, I have one invaluable piece of advice. Do not be scared of resignation letters. If someone submits a resignation letter, accept it without a question. You will be surprised to find how many of them just use the resignation letter as a negotiation tactic. They consider themselves so invaluable that they assume you would immediately bend over backward to fulfill their demands. It could be an outlandish raise or a promotion that they do not deserve. I have seen many letters of consternation following the letters of resignation.

You have to understand that if a person submits a resignation letter, they have fired a bullet. Once the bullet is out of the chamber, you cannot force it back into the gun. They have just tried to blackmail you to get a better deal for themselves. So, accept the resignation. Another key message lies in the word itself: Resignation! There will be people who offer their resignation because they genuinely want to quit and not as a negotiation tactic. It just means they are resigned to the fact that there is nothing they can do in the company to get their grievances addressed. In such cases, the fault may be found on both sides. So, if you receive a resignation letter from anyone, accept it. You want motivated and energetic people in your company. You do not want wily or weary staff members. It does not matter what positions they hold in the company.

I repeat, do not be scared of resignation letters. As far as I am concerned, it is good riddance. I have also come across other unique pressures. I remember getting a call one day. The caller said he was from the Prime Minister's Office. I was surprised.

When I inquired about the purpose of the call, he told me that he wanted me to rehire a person who had been let go. I refused. Over the years, I have received calls from people purporting to be from the PMO, Delhi Police, Economic Offences Wing, Central Bureau of Investigation, and offices of MPs and MLAs. They all tried to pressure me into rehiring people who had been sacked. You will be subject to many such pressures. I understand and appreciate that such pressures can be a scary prospect. I have been threatened by these callers that they would shut me down if I did not rehire those people. I refused to bend. There is no space for nepotism. It is your company, your baby. You should be able to hire and fire people as you see fit. Just follow the laws; ensure compensation as per the law.

There have been quite a few learnings that I wish to share with you in my years dealing with the labor force and with people. The first thing to remember is that if you wish to go far, you cannot do it alone. You need people who wish to march with you and match your cadence. Do not become narrow-minded and focus only on personal short-term profits. Invest in your employees. Become a mentor and champion their causes. Celebrate and relish their successes. Commiserate with them on their losses. Take pride in their growth. Their growth and achievements do not minimize your goals. Their successes will only magnify your successes.

There is a paraphrased John F Kennedy quote—Ask not what your country can do for you, ask what you can do for your country. I do not bring back this quote to inspire any feelings of patriotism or jingoism. I have only referenced it to highlight one significant aim for an entrepreneur. Focus on what you can do for others and not what they can do for you. As I mentioned earlier, I have come across many people who dread salary days. They detest having to pay their employees. They begrudgingly pay their employees.

Such people have lost the focus of having a motivated workforce. When you look to contribute more, you will find that the workforce will be more motivated to work with you and achieve your combined goals. Such endeavors will only lead to greater satisfaction and fulfillment.

There is a misconception that you can only contribute to workforce morale in monetary terms. However, this would only form part of the jigsaw puzzle. Good leadership is essential to having a good labor force. This may lead you to ask how you can be a good leader? I have already spoken about the monetary aspect. Do not miss paying your employees.

However, there are a few fundamental aspects of leadership that you should not ignore. You may be surprised by how simple and obvious many of these aspects may seem, but many people either forget or ignore them. The first aspect is that you set clear expectations. Your workforce should know what they are expected to do and what constitutes a good job. Recognize their efforts when they do a good job. It can be a simple acknowledgment, but it can be quite the potent reinforcement.

People want to do a good job and recognizing their efforts can provide them a form of satisfaction that even money cannot provide. Just imagine a scenario, where you are being paid two or three times your current salary. However, there is a caveat. You would be subjected to a daily berating of how you have not done a good job. To complicate matters further, your boss never tells you what you should do to ensure a good job.

If you ask that question, you will be subjected to further abuse for not knowing. Crucially, the boss never tells you what is a good job. Would you take up such a job? The money may seem very attractive in the beginning. However, the allure will soon be dispelled and you will find that the extra money is not worth the stress. So, as a leader, be clear about your expectations and let your workforce know what is a good job, and commend them when they do it. Speaking of expectations, ensure that they are repeated and modified over time. The world is dynamic and it is understood that the expectations will change. Keep your workforce updated on the changes and keep them abreast of how their roles have changed. If you find a lack in performance, do not fly off the handle immediately. If you look at most performance problems, you will see that it is not down to a lack in performance.

They can be traced to a lack of awareness of the expectations. They may not be aware of how their roles have changed. For instance, a manager may have been able to successfully drive their department because they had a finger on the pulse. It is possible for the manager to be successful if the team is small. However, what happens when the team expands following explosive growth? The same manager will not be able to deliver the same results if they stick to the same micromanagement process. So, a leader has to ensure that the concerned manager is made aware of their responsibilities.

I challenge you to ask people who have worked for a while about whom they consider as the best leader. Ask them what made such leaders special. They could be people from varying profiles and experiences. They all may name different people. Some may talk of their first boss or the current boss. However, there will be one commonality to all the answers. It will be in the way they answer the second question: What made them special? They may tell you different stories and use different words. However, it would boil down to one essence: They cared.

They genuinely cared about their employees. They become special not because of their technical expertise or knowledge. They become special because they cared. It is vital that as a leader you genuinely care for your workforce. If you were to think about it, we dedicate so much of our lives to work. It can dictate so much of our lives. Would people want to spend it where they are not valued? Appreciate your workforce.

Treat them as human beings and not instruments that produce your profit. Be committed to their welfare and you will see that your labor force will embrace you and your company more wholeheartedly.

There are bound to be bad eggs, and you can see from my story that there will be people who will not be swayed by your care. However, my experience for the most part is that people respond with commitment and effort when you are genuine in your care for them. They become long-term followers who will accomplish far more than expected when they are recognized for their work.

One of the fundamental aspects of effective leadership is effective feedback. Feedback is vital to the development of employees. It helps them understand their weaknesses and mistakes and work on them. If used correctly, feedback can build the confidence of the workforce. However, it does not mean that you are constantly checking and providing feedback. Timing is the key here. Use positive language and pick the right time and place. If you constantly push for providing feedback, it could be like the case of the boy who cried wolf. Your feedback will cease to have any effect on your workforce.

Nit-picking is different from feedback. The former becomes a distraction and negatively affects employee morale. It shows a lack of trust and builds an environment of hostility and defensiveness. As a leader, I look for only one thing when it comes to providing feedback. It should serve in making the employee become better. It is not about positioning myself to feel superior and better than others. A thumb rule that I follow when it comes to providing feedback is that it should be specific and actionable. If my feedback is vague, I hold my opinion until I am sure that I have specific, actionable input to provide.

Feedback can help build an environment that fosters open lines of communication and cooperation. Such an environment is critical as it can help people thrive. Such environments have clear expectations and feature genuine and authentic connections. I cannot stress this enough—be present in your connections and relationships. If you were to walk down the road today, you will find people immersed in technology via their earphones and headphones. If you walk into a restaurant, you may see people come with their family or friends.

You will see their table laden with the most delicious food. However, you would most likely also be distracted by the numerous flashes of light as people snap pictures to be uploaded with the best filters on their social media pages. I spoke of how technology has evolved. Gone are the days when I hunted for the phone line technicians to prioritize my phone line in Tughlaqabad.

Technology has brought us closer when it comes to communication, but this convenience has come with its own cost. People have taken their connection with others a bit too lightly. So, as a leader, you cannot do the same.

It is vital that you build personable connections. It may not have the same intimacy as that of a personal relationship with a spouse or a sibling. However, be present in every connection. When you are speaking or listening to someone, be present in that conversation. Show them that you value your time with them. It could be a business partner, a friend, or a spouse. It does not matter. Be with them at that moment. Do not let your mind stray in chase of vagrant thoughts and or move away at a tangent. Put your mobile phone away and be present in the moment.

However, there are certain things you need to keep in mind when it comes to hiring and firing employees. It is vital that you land the correct hires when it comes to the key positions. There can be only one endgame. You should not even entertain the idea of hiring mediocre staff. You have no other choice but to get it right. However, if you find out that you have hired a terrible person among your first hires, fire them. Do not even hesitate as such team members can be cancerous to the growth of your company. If you have worries or doubts regarding firing them, remind yourself that the survival of your company is at stake. Look out for signs of passive-aggressiveness. Such people can bring the morale down and demotivate everyone.

Some employers might find it difficult to fire people. My advice would be to find and build your intestinal fortitude. Do not fool yourself into thinking that a person you have deemed to be terrible for the company can improve. I have to disabuse you of this notion. Such people never improve.

They may have regrets down the line, but they will not look for improvement. As a leader, ensure that you build and nurture a team that constantly looks to improve and can be productive. It is at this juncture that I have to speak about the core values of your organization.

Some of you may have seen companies paint their vision and mission statements on the walls of their premises. It may seem unnecessary. However, such paintings are a reminder to all of the core values of your company. If you are not sure of your core values, you will find it hard to differentiate between good and terrible employees. At *Saivana*, Vandana has been a driving force when it comes to the soul of our company. I have been able to draw associated values in marketing and other departments around her ideas. We now hire and fire workers based on those core values.

It is also vital that you have a proper interview process. Your interview process should be able to separate the wheat from the chaff. If you come across candidates for whom you would like to give the benefit of the doubt, it means that your interview process is not robust enough. Design your interview questions to help you arrive at the best possible candidate. It can be a simple question that holds the key.

I found mine by asking people about their greatest failures and how they picked themselves up from that fall. It is a simple question but has tripped many people when they were looking to portray a pseudo image of perfection rather than a disposition to learn and evolve. There have been cases where some candidates may have had great resumes with extensive experience and yet stumbled at that question. Another key aspect to remember is that you do not blindly take anyone at their word. I have been burned badly by many people who abused that trust and faith. Repose your trust in people who have delivered for a long period of time. However, it would be ideal if you keep revisiting these trust relationships once in a while. Test their calibration and evaluate them.

Extra Customization:

- To eliminate any form of nepotism in senior staff positions, I do the entire hiring process myself. My HR staff vet the resumes for the other positions. It is not that I do not trust my staff; it is that I trust myself to do a better job.

- I have come across people who lied on their resumes that they were being paid Rs 80,000 per month. I would have negotiated a salary package of Rs 75,000 and feel proud that I saved Rs 5000. However, a few months later, I would discover that they were actually paid only Rs 30,000. It is one of the reasons why we conduct background checks on all our potential new hires.

- Over the years, *Saivana* has seen at least six protests and strikes called against it. People unfurled red flags and demonstrated in front of my factory. They hurled the choicest abuses and even burned my effigy. There was both air pollution and noise pollution with all the smoke and sound. However, I was also slightly disappointed that the effigies just carried my name! They did not even resemble me in the slightest. They did not even carry my picture. They just bore my name, Rajat Sikka. These statements are in jest. But I have always been wary of such tumultuous labor issues. Over time, I learned the laws of the land. I came to know that the protestors could not demonstrate in front of my factory. They had to keep a distance of 100 meters from the factory. This legality was one of the many things I picked up in a steep learning curve over the years.

- Seventeen years after the first labor dispute, the remorseful union leader who was once my right-hand man called to apologize. He also wanted me to help him find a new job. I cut him off as I have never forgiven him for almost killing me and *Saivana*.

- I have two theories when it comes to internal white-collar corruption. The first is that be wary of people who become fatter, especially if they start developing the famous Indian beer belly. Be especially careful if they are from the accounts department.

Investigate, and you will most likely find that they are eating into your company profits. My second theory is that you have to be careful of people who never take a holiday.

While you may think such work ethic is worth commending, the truth is that you will only find the problem when they stop coming in to work. Them not taking a holiday means they are the scariest when they take a day off. On their day off, you will find the scams they ran in their departments. Another noticeable trait is when they do not have effective seconds-in-command. This may not necessarily mean corruption, but it certainly indicates to their sense of insecurity in their jobs.

- We had problems with betel stains not just on the clothes, but also on the walls of the factory. We tried several schemes. We designed a facial mask in-house for the staff. But it failed. We came across a solution to stop people spitting on the walls when we painted religious imagery on the walls. People stopped spitting on the walls. But I wish some chemical company could make a product to remove these stains.

- The name *Saivana* has a spiritual context. The originally planned name was Savana. It was an amalgamation of Sikka and Vandana. I called a friend to find out where I could get business cards printed. I told him the name of my company was Savana. He misheard it as *Saivana* and remarked, "Hey Rajat! That is wonderful that you are naming your business after Sai Baba." I was surprised but thought that the name certainly made sense and hoped that it would also appease my mother who was a devotee of Shirdi Sai Baba. That is how *Saivana* came into existence! What a remarkable thing it was! It was as if Sai Baba himself had ensured that the company was named after him. If this is not a miracle, what else could it be?

Sai Baba and Vandana have been the magic trick. There is no way I could have carried this on my own. If she was not there, I would have carried on like a typical Punjabi businessman. People would have taken advantage of my lack of expertise and knowledge in this area. Nobody could fool Vandana in this regard. Sai Baba's blessings have ensured that we have been able to come out of every challenge stronger.

"The function of leadership is to produce more leaders, not more followers."

- Ralph Nader

6
AAP PEOPLE GHERAO ME

"The more corrupt the state, the more numerous the laws." — Tacitus,
The Annals of Imperial Rome

I have come across many news headlines and reports saying that the ease of doing business in India has improved. I find that proposition a bit funny. I am not casting any aspersions toward any government. I wonder who draws the markers and measurements to say that the ease of doing business in India has improved. One of the toughest things to do in India is to start and run a manufacturing business.

You will be subject to constant harassment from various departments. It can be a thankless task to deal with the number of inspectors involved. You could be following every detail as per the law, but there will still be some loopholes that the inspector will exploit. In the latter half of the first decade of *Saivana*, I spent every day dealing with inspectors. I was once again diverted away from my core business to deal with these inspections and the inspectors involved. *Saivana* has always gone by the book and is transparent in its transactions. However, it is not possible to follow every law to the letter. Let me give you an example.

As mandated by law, every factory in India must have two entrances and exits for emergency use. My factory had all those exits. However, one of the exit doors would lead into the back wall of a jhuggi. A jhuggi is an illegal house that you commonly associate with slum dwellings. It is typically made out of corrugated iron and mud.

So, we had to keep that door closed. One day, an inspector came to inspect the premises. He verified that our factory adhered to all the protocols. He then asked to check the emergency exits. He was finally led to the closed door. We unlocked the door and showed him the jhuggi that was blocking it. He immediately said that there was a violation. He said that the locked door was a violation of the protocol. I tried to reason with him. I told him the violation was clearly due to the illegal construction of a house. That construction was out of my hands. I had no control over it. I cannot remove the jhuggi of my own accord. I would only invite the wrath of the local people for demolishing someone's residence. But my pleas fell on deaf ears. The inspector wrote up a report. The result: I had to send someone to the court again to pay the fine.

I have lost count of the number of times I have had to send employees to the court to pay fines for frivolous complaints filed by the inspectors. However, the greatest source of frustration comes from the local municipal corporations. They can harass you beyond all limits of tolerance. I remember a recent incident where I was shocked by the local municipal corporation's claim. One of their representatives came to me and told me that there was a problem with my property tax filings.

I was surprised as I had never defaulted on any such payments. We paid the property taxes on our factories without fail and had no arrears. The man explained to me and told me that I had paid the property tax by declaring that the factory had an area of 2500 square feet. However, when the corporation measured the area, the actual area was found to be 2505 square feet. He then accounted for the additional five square feet over the period of 20 years and factored in fines and interest payments. His final demand, *Saivana* had an arrear of Rs 1.5 crore.

The harassment from local authorities was so severe that I had to assign two or three people just to negotiate with them. One of the more surprising incidents was being informed that I needed to obtain a special license just to park our vehicles in front of our factory.

I refused to pay any fine for not having the license. I explained to them that we were parking in front of our premises. Why did we need a special license? When my refusal was conveyed to the local municipal corporation, it was as if I had summoned the fury of the gods. The parking sub-contractor, the municipal corporation representative, and even a parking inspector from the local corporation descended on me inquiring why I had not paid the parking fees. It was only on that day I came to know that there was a specially designated parking inspector!

I have been frustrated by these innumerable inspections. There were occasions when I was sorely tempted to deliver some well-deserved (in my opinion) slaps to these inspectors. These people have never bothered about the ground realities of the situation.

I have to be especially wary around Diwali. All these people expect gifts, and if you forget any one person, you will be experiencing the wrong kind of fireworks. I could not fathom how they could be so malicious. Their favorite threat was they would close me down. Just imagine, I was employing over 100 people, and most of them were sole breadwinners of their families. Then some inspector would saunter in and expect me to give him a cut. How could he so easily threaten to disrupt proceedings and endanger so many workers' livelihood?

He is supposed to be a public servant, yet how can he consider the public with such callous disregard? Some of the reasons can be so flimsy; I do not know how they can use it without the slightest cringe. Let me give you another example. The signboard outside my factory says *Saivana*. However, the registered name with the government is Saivana Exports Pvt. Ltd. Since I did not display the full name of my company on the signboard, it became a violation and the factory could be shut down.

Inspectors in India can be very rigid! I dread when the festivals of Diwali and Holi roll around. This can be an extremely trying time as the local inspectors come calling in advance. These experiences are akin to having your teeth extracted without anesthesia. The callers will try to extract as much as they can from you. If you need some advice to avoid such constant harassment, I would say, "Stay still." Remain small, and they will not bother you as much. The key words being 'as much.' There is a direct correlation between growth and the frequency of inspector visits. I am not out to dissuade you from being ambitious. I am asking you to steel yourself for trouble when you grow.

The inspectors will find one loophole to extract as many teeth as they can. I was once accosted by the property tax inspector. He told me that I was robbing the exchequer of India. I showed him the documents and receipts that proved that I had paid the property taxes on time without default. However, he pounced on one loophole. He told me that I had paid industrial property tax. I was a bit flummoxed.

Saivana was a garment manufacturer and so would fall within the ambit of industrial property. I explained it to him and was wondering if he did not understand the definition of garment manufacturing. He was unmoved. He told me that there was something I had not declared. He pointed to my office wall and said, "This room and the entire floor is office space. There is no manufacturing on this floor. So, this floor is a commercial space."

Commercial property taxes are higher than industrial property taxes. Once more, I was given an outrageous amount after the inspector's calculation. I am still perplexed by this problem. How can a factory work without an office? Where was I supposed to sit? Do I appropriate a sewing machine to use as my table? How should the staff who handle documents work? Did I need to place a sewing machine in each of the office rooms to make the office space also an industrial space? I always had the option to report such corrupt inspectors to the concerned authorities. I would learn later, to my detriment, that the inspectors can be a vengeful bunch.

If I reported one inspector, a horde of them would descend on my factory and find a litany of frivolous issues to write out a challan. You report one inspector, and you are bound to be inspected far more stringently by the remaining inspectors.

There is one more reason why going to the authorities can be painful. Once, an inspector came to my office and asked to see the factory license. He had done his inspections and wanted one last check. He checked the factory license and hinted that he was waiting for his gift. I refused as he had not identified any faults and we had passed his inspection. He shook his head and had an expression that said I would come to regret it. A few days later, we received the customary mail following the inspection. We had been summoned to the court to pay a fine, and the reason given was that we had not shown the inspector our factory license.

What was I supposed to do in this situation? It was clearly a case of his word against mine. I could not go to court as I was meeting a prospective buyer who could give us a huge order. I was so anticipatory of the deal that even the blatant lie by the inspector did not hold me down for long. As usual, I sent one of my staff members to the court on the assigned date.

I pushed the issue to the back of my mind expecting it to proceed as usual. The powder keg was lit when one of my administrative staff came into my room during my meeting with the potential client. He was apprehensive, but he told me that the court had summoned me personally. I was informed that if I did not present myself to the court within an hour, a non-bailable arrest warrant would be issued. I was afforded no choice. I had to, regrettably, end the meeting and rush to the court. It certainly was not the ideal first impression. However, I went to the court and presented myself.

The court asked me if I had refused to show the license. They asked me if I even possessed one in the first place. I patiently explained to the judge that my factory was in Okhla. I would not have been permitted to do anything if I did not have a license. I then presented my license to the court. Thankfully, the court saw to it that justice was served and threw out the case.

However, the repercussions were felt elsewhere. I lost the client because of my court visit. Here, it was the case of the inspector's word against mine. I lost an important deal because I had to go to court one afternoon.

What if I pursued this case to the full extent? How many days would I have had to spend in the courts! There will also be exorbitant lawyer fees to contend with in these cases. How many hours would I have wasted in this endeavor? I lost a business deal because of that one afternoon; what would I lose by being embroiled in a legal battle?

As I have suffered through these circumstances, I find the idea laughable that the ease of doing business in India has improved. The 'inspector raaj' is alive. However, I must stress that I have come across many brilliant inspectors. Some IAS officers and officials at the Customs Office have been nothing but upright and honest. They are prompt to reply and respond in case of any grievances. There have been occasions where we had to visit the Customs Office because somebody would have held back our rightful due because of the duty-back scheme of the government. There are excellent inspectors with the needed moral fiber. But they are few and far between. Worryingly, they are found only at the national level.

The 'inspector raaj' is prevalent at the local and state level. These inspectors appear as the typical caricatures of Bollywood corrupt police. They are obese, chew tobacco, and boast of how they can shut you down.

While I may have a lot of complaints against the inspectors, I know why they are needed. Are there businesses that cut corners? Yes. I would be a fool to say otherwise. However, they represent a minority.

They could constitute about two percent of the businesses in India, but the remaining 98 percent of businesses have to bear the brunt of the oppression and bullying by inspectors. As entrepreneurs, we should be seen as creators of employment opportunities. However, when the inspectors come visiting, we are treated as if we are venomous capitalists.

We are treated as if we only want to exploit the labor force. My experience with inspectors has been that, often, they are the opposite of what they purport themselves to be.

They are supposed to be the ones who are looking out for the welfare of the public. They are instead looking out only for themselves.

I can say this with a good deal of confidence that if three young aspiring fashion designers decide to start a garment manufacturing company today, they will fold up within the year. Such is the harassment of inspectors. If you are an entrepreneur, steady yourself. You will need incredible mental resilience and patience to deal with such bullies.

There will be more than one occasion when you would want to cut loose. There will be moments when you will be engulfed in rage and frustration. There will be moments when you would want to beat the inspector within an inch of his life. I had struck such rock-bottom more than once.

My employees have had to hold me back from worsening my situation. There will also be moments when you feel impotent as they blatantly boast of their power. However, you will need all your patience to tide over those troubled waters. Develop your resilience and patience. Also, prepare a lot of Diwali gifts!

Extra customization:

- One of my priorities was to build a wall of protection for Vandana from these inspectors. I wanted her to focus on the garments and their designs. I became the wall. However, I had to hire and assign staff to build a wall between myself and the inspectors with each deteriorating circumstance. My aim was to protect Vandana and let her operate from her zone of genius, designing. As I mentioned earlier, the whole company revolved around her and her expertise. I knew we could not afford to let her be bogged down by these issues and hence handled them on my own.

- One of the ironic inspection visits was when an inspector came into the factory to check the Air Quality Index (AQI) within the premises. I wanted to ask him if he had checked the AQI outside the factory. Delhi's AQI is so bad that we failed the inspection even with the best air purifiers.

- Did you know that if you need to install a generator on your premises, you need to get a license? If you do not obtain a license to do so, your factory is liable to be shut down.

- I was once informed by an inspector that I could not have an office space in the basement. Apparently, as per Delhi local law, the basement can only be used as a storage space. However, how many lawyers and doctors operate out of basements in Delhi? I have lost count.

- One of the biggest issues is that the law in India is constantly changing and being revised. It can be hard to keep track of the changes. However, the inspectors come in armed with this new knowledge and have you trapped. Due to the many revisions, invariably, you will not have followed a rule at some point.

- There have been occasions when I have been told a certain inspector is a straight shooter. I wanted to commend such an inspector. I wanted to start a new Nobel prize for honesty and give him the award. However, I would later find out that he was a straight shooter in the sense that he was more straightforward in asking for gifts, and his price used to be even more expensive.

- The local municipal corporation has over 20 departments. You may be visited by an inspector on Monday, and after sorting the issue, you may assume the matter is settled.

On Wednesday, an inspector from another department will visit you for another issue. There have been occasions when the inspectors send their juniors or seniors for their share of gifts. I have also come across a few retired inspectors who come in for their gifts even after they have retired from public service.

There were also a couple of inspectors who visited my factory after a period of five years. They wanted gifts retrospectively!

- I have also been questioned at ports for being exploitative. As we catered to clients in the higher tier of fashion, some people have balked at our quoted prices. Some officials even wondered as to why we were charging such high rates. But thankfully, excellent IRS and IAS officers bailed us out by understanding that we were producing high-value garments.

- I do not know how exactly to combat this 'inspector raaj.' The first investigation should be about how much salary the local municipal corporations are paying these inspectors. If they are being paid a pittance, it would explain why they have to resort to such tactics to make more money. It does not justify their actions, but there is an explanation. Another tactic could be to reduce the number of licenses and requirements needed to establish and run a business. You need about 40 to 50 licenses just to start a manufacturing business. If we could reduce the number of requirements, it could lead to fewer inspections. A rule is to be set that an inspector cannot fine you for flimsy reasons. If we could revisit the factory license case, what are the repercussions for the inspector? It will help if such checks and balances are instituted.

"The price of success is hard work, dedication to the job at hand, and the determination that whether we win or lose, we have applied the best of ourselves to the task at hand."

- Vince Lombardi

7
BOSTON CLAM CHOWDER

"We tend to overvalue the things we can measure and undervalue the things we cannot." — John Hayes

How can a husband-and-wife team work together in harmony? It is often argued that husband and wife cannot work together because there is bound to be friction at the workplace. That friction often spills onto the home front. It invariably does. A bad day at work translates to a bad day at home. That is why you rarely see successful husband and wife partnerships.

When running a business as a husband-and-wife partnership, it is a given that you would encounter differences of opinion and clashes. In our case, my wife was in charge of the production and technical aspects of garment manufacturing while I was in charge of strategy and marketing. Our roles had to go hand in hand for *Saivana* to prosper.

There were countless clashes between Vandana and myself. She was a hands-on type of manager, while I was the opposite. You need to be hands-on when you are in garment manufacturing. However, there is no room for micromanaging. I could see the toll it was taking on the business, and I knew we needed some perspective.

As mentioned earlier, my wife came from a fashion background. We realized the need for her to gain some management perspectives. She needed to be able to delegate tasks. The year was 2008. We came across a course offered by Harvard Business School (HBS). The course was called the Owners-Presidents- Management (OPM) program.

As the name indicates, the course was offered to owners, presidents, and management executives of small to medium-sized business enterprises.

The course was designed to help these individuals take their company to the next level. We realized that this was our manna from heaven. Thus, in 2008, my wife enrolled in this program. It was tough going for her in the beginning. There was the inevitable homesickness and other related issues in the first few days. She was facing an entirely new atmosphere far removed from our Delhi factory. She was in one of the premier business schools in the world, with a wide range of businesspersons in her class. There were people who were far more experienced, and then there were the tyros with burning ambition.

It was an eclectic mix of students and proved to be a fertile ground for discussion and debate. Vandana overcame her initial hesitation after she made a few good friends, and the course did wonders for her. I flew to Boston for her graduation. I could see a transformational change in her.

She was calmer and more open to the delegation of work and embraced her management role. I was curious to see how this change had come about. She spoke to one of her professors, and I got a wonderful opportunity. I got the chance to sit in for two classes and audit them. I wanted to know what the secret ingredient was. After having sat through the two classes, there was one overriding thought in my mind. This course would be equally useful for me as well, or maybe more so. I too needed to take the course.

So, four years later, in 2012, I enrolled in the course as well. I had seen the changes in my wife over the four years since she took the course.

It would be shortchanging the course to call it a game-changer for *Saivana*. As far as I was concerned, it was a life-changer for Vandana and me. The OPM program is spread across three modules. The first module is three weeks long. You spend that time on the Harvard Business School campus. Then you get a break of one year. You can apply the learnings from the first module over that one year. Then you have another module for another three weeks.

It is followed by another year-long break, and you go for the final module for three more weeks. The course is designed with a clear intention. Change, especially organizational change, takes time. You cannot wish it overnight. You have to encourage and motivate employees across lines to effect such changes.

Those nine weeks are packed with so much information and education that you, as the company leader, will need time to digest and reflect upon it. Hence, the three weeks module followed by a year-long break can see you experiment with different strategies. You can find which ideas work for you and which ideas may need tweaking.

The lessons we learned from Harvard were both inside the classroom and outside. In my class, there were entrepreneurs from 160 countries with students from India, Brazil, and the USA dominating the student body. Our class was a great mix of people from varied backgrounds. We had one person who owned one of the largest funeral service companies in Spain. Morbid as it may sound, we thought it was a fantastic business because he would never be short on customers as death and taxes have been ordained on all by God.

We had a grandmother from India who wanted to learn more so that she could contribute to her family's home furnishings business. She just went on to prove the point that age is no barrier when it comes to learning.

The youngest in our group eagerly told us about a new tech product. He called it Bitcoin. I remember we all were so cynical about it. It seemed like mumbo jumbo to us and little did we realize that this would become a potent economic force in the future.

If only we had not dismissed our young colleague so lightly, who, if I might add, went on to become one of the most successful business people from our whole class.

The first three weeks at Harvard were the most interesting. It was as if we had entered a new world and it felt like the professors were going to provide us with all the tools to solve our problems back home. For me, it was a big refreshing change from Delhi society as I listened to the success stories of my peers.

I remember one class when the professor asked us a question. He wanted to know which companies of the representatives in the class were not making money and one hand went up. After class, I met the guy who had raised his hand and told him politely how sorry I was to hear his company was not making money. He casually shrugged and said, "Yes, but you know my company is listed on NASDAQ and the valuation is close to a billion dollars." To say I kind of choked is putting it mildly.

While I made friends mostly from among those in my class, I became very close to the people in my first unit. The concept of HBS was that seven to eight people would live in their individual rooms but share a common living room where everyday cases would be discussed.

Those were the first days of Harvard and I just loved my living room group. We had one guy from South Africa, one from Mexico, two Americans, one from Thailand, and including me, we were two from India. Our group was one of the best (I know, I can just visualize people from other groups saying, "What nonsense!"). One of the Americans actually flew in on his private plane from New Orleans to Boston.

Later on, in Unit 2, I realized my dream of flying a plane when I sat with my friend as his co-pilot and we flew to Lake Placid for a weekend getaway. It was exhilarating, to say the least. I also made some great friends among my fellow countrymen, and to date, all my HBS OPM friends feel like a part of my family. Whenever we meet, no matter how long it has been, it is always with a great deal of respect, fun, and warmth.

A special shout out to my Harvard Boys buddies who are always willing to help at the drop of a hat and with whom I have had some great times in Goa, Dubai, and Kerala, post-Harvard.

The cases studies at Harvard were brilliant. One of the personal branding cases we had was on the famous supermodel Tyra Banks and she visited the classroom in person. That was the only day I sat in the front row for any class, much to the amusement of my classmates. But the learning was tremendous. From that case, I learned that *Saivana* by itself was a brand.

Sure, it was not a Brand-to-Customer brand (B2C), but rather it was a Brand-to-Business (B2B) one. I had to look at *Saivana* as a brand and how it was important to its stakeholders, from buyers to workers to suppliers. I immediately tasked myself to find out the brand attributes of *Saivana*. I was shocked.

While we thought we were the top guns in our industry, some of our buyers thought otherwise. "*Saivana* is always late," "*Saivana* is too expensive," "Too much politics in *Saivana*," etc., were some of the frequent responses. Yes, there were some good things also said but I was more concerned about the negative brand attributes. Changing a brand perception is not easy and it takes time. But Vandana and I then decided that we had to change the perception as negativity can really affect a brand and its selling power.

We slowly started implementing policies at the floor levels of our factory in order to improve our deliveries. Proper planning systems were put in place and the importance of on-time deliveries was inoculated into the minds of each of the key employees of *Saivana* through training and lectures. At the same time, we initiated cost-cutting measures in order to bring our prices down. It was not done immediately but it took a lot of hard work. To change the mindset of the workforce is difficult and any owner wanting to initiate change will have to grind their way and put in the hours to make change happen.One of the most interesting aspects taught at Harvard was about negotiating. From an early age, I had been a poor negotiator. On the other hand, my aunt would not need a crash course at the best university in the world to learn about negotiations.

I remember going to the fruit market with her when I was a child, and when the shopkeeper said that the apples were Rs 50 per kilogram, my aunt used to firmly say, "No, Rs 5 a kilogram." I used to be very embarrassed by her bargaining.

I mean there was a huge difference between Rs 50 and Rs 5 and there was no way this gap could be bridged. Much to my astonishment, my aunt used to triumphantly walk out with a bag of apples bought at Rs 7 per kilogram.

I, on the other hand, would have been happy to buy them at Rs 30 per kilogram and would have given myself a pat on the back for a job well done. How was she able to do it? A) She knew what the current prices were. B) She knew what her budget was. C) She knew he would sell at Rs 7 per kilogram. D) He was making a fool of her by quoting Rs 50 per kilogram in the first place. Harvard taught us pretty much the same thing but in a more formal and structured manner. These learnings have helped me tremendously in various business negotiations. However, as a word of caution, these negotiation tactics do not work when it comes to dealing with loved ones or relatives.

The most significant lesson I got from the OPM course happened to be in one of the first few classes. The professor came and asked us what should be the focus for any entrepreneur. Many of us came up with the same answer or some variation of it. It was about financial investment, financial prudence, maximizing profitability, etc. They all revolved around the idea of Return on Investment (RoI). It was understandable as we were all small and medium-sized enterprises. Our ideas of scaling new heights involved increasing our revenues and thus profits. However, the professor gave us a reality check. He told us that focusing on the RoI would severely limit our growth as entrepreneurs. He wanted us to focus on RoL instead. He explained that RoL stood for Return on Life. He asked us to reflect on our life and business. Are there any situations that are affecting your life? Are you frustrated? Do some of these situations or activities create stress in your life? Do you find yourself stuck in bouts of anger or tears?

All of these negatively affect your RoL. He talked of how we only had one life to live. So, it was necessary to remove all stress points from our lives. I remember a line he said during the class. He said that coffins do not have pockets. You cannot carry anything once you are dead. So, why were we subjecting ourselves to miserable lives with the primary focus on wealth generation?

The next fundamental lesson that I drew from the course was the importance of having a succession plan in place. I knew the importance of this immediately. I had already been to court several times against my family and loved ones. My father had passed away without having a proper succession plan in place. The lawsuits had wrecked the relationships I had with my family. When I returned from Harvard, my wife and I were in agreement.

We have two daughters, and we did not want them to go down the same path that we had. So, we decided that they would share everything equally. The professor had a few more wise words for why having a succession plan was needed. First, it was imperative that we do not leave a legacy of debt and confusion. There is a famous adage of how the child pays for the sins of the father. However, it is up to the father that he does not leave such a burden on his children.

The second idea brought us back to the RoL concept. He explained how we could make money for ourselves and our children. However, we cannot dictate how the generations after spend that money. So, why do you need to toil to make obscene amounts of money? The RoL concept asks for us to enjoy life and be self-sufficient.

The next important lesson from our Harvard excursions was the importance of making ourselves redundant from the business. Trust me, you have not read that statement wrongly! One of the biggest mistakes entrepreneurs make is to be immersed in their business. Let us take the example of my area of work. Garment manufacturers work all seven days of the week. They can get extremely worried if they miss a day. They fear that their absence, even for a day, would spell disaster for their company.

They worry that the company would not be able to function without them and that it will result in the company becoming a dumpster fire. I sympathize with their views as I entertained similar thoughts prior to Harvard. One of the earliest decisions that Vandana and I took after Harvard was to step back on weekends. We decided that the weekends would be our time.

We would spend it with our daughters and use the weekend to completely take a break from work. When people came to know of our plan, they were flabbergasted. It was as if our proposal was heresy. They could not understand how we could even think along those lines.

I remember the first Saturday that Vandana and I stopped going to the factory. I received around 22 calls from different levels of the company. They needed my direction to sort some issue or the other. On Monday, my first action on reaching the office was to summon those 22 callers. I fined each of them Rs 500.

I asked them how they could breach into my personal time. I had never reached out to them for anything during their holidays and off-days unless it was an express emergency. The fines were collected and put into the Diwali party fund for the employees. However, I had laid down the marker. I have never received a call on the weekends ever since. There was an immediate lesson for me from that weekend. I had involved myself in the practices and protocols to an extent that my employees had lost their autonomy. They became dependent upon Vandana or me to make decisions at every level.

The employees also got another benefit from our absences on the weekends. Saturdays became a relaxed workday. It became days where they could hold internal meetings and use them to vent their frustrations and take decisions that would enhance their effectiveness and efficiency. Naturally, they will not be relaxed when the big bosses are around. There will be a wall of reservation that will be extremely hard to overcome. If there is one lesson we can learn from the Western world as entrepreneurs, it is their work culture. People have five-day or four-day workweeks.

However, given the nature of the business, I cannot extend the same benefit to my employees. Instead, what Vandana and I did was to take longer breaks. We wanted them to work in a relaxed work atmosphere. It was our contribution to their RoL. However, there is a greater need for entrepreneurs to make themselves redundant to their business.

I want to clarify one point here: Redundancy does not indicate uselessness to the business. When I say redundant, entrepreneurs need to divorce themselves from the daily operations. If they are mired in the daily grind, where will they find time to strategize for long-term growth? It is imperative to see the forest from the trees. For that vision, you need a bird's eye view.

You need to figure out where your company stands in the broader picture. Is there an area that the company wants to explore? How about new markets or new buyers? How about new suppliers? If you are stuck in the operations, you will never find these avenues.

If you are an entrepreneur, I will simply advise you to start by taking one Saturday off. Would your company burn to the ground if you took that day off? Begin from that point and see how you and your workforce can blossom. In your absence, you can find leaders who will step up.

They will cherish the responsibilities given to them. In their newfound freedom, they will take up initiatives that will help your company grow in strength. You will then find a more committed workforce and a natural succession policy within the company. If an executive steps down or moves to newer pastures, you may not need to headhunt people outside. There will be people capable enough within your organization to step up and take charge.

We saw the greatest benefit of removing ourselves from the daily operations during the COVID pandemic. The team we had nurtured stepped up to the plate during this time. They figured out solutions and carried them out flawlessly. There were indeed some people who could not cope, and we had to let them go. But most of my employees figured out ways to work, and they did so efficiently with minimum fuss.

On a related note, there was another thing that I did after I returned from Harvard. I fired the big talkers from the company. I did not want people who only talked but balked from the action. It did not matter where they were in the organization's hierarchy. I fired my CFO and four to five other key people from the hierarchy. They all got their marching orders.

I then found many leaders within *Saivana*, as I mentioned earlier. I promoted them, and it has only helped *Saivana* march forward into the future with courage and grace. Many of those promoted personnel are still with *Saivana* and hold high positions. A case study can be done on how these promoted youngsters coped with the pressures and blossomed. I can say this with great confidence— empower the youth of this country. Entrust them with responsibility, and they will take up the mantle and make you proud. I saw that in *Saivana*, and they have never failed to live up to my lofty expectations. Many of them even transcended those expectations.

There will be some bad apples, sure; but the vast majority of people are honest and loyal. One of the lessons I learned from *Saivana* is that experience does not count as much as loyalty. When you can make the youth within your company loyal and steadfast to your company, they will deliver. You can do so by paying them well and giving them opportunities and responsibilities to grow further. Do not be suspicious of them. So, try and make yourself redundant from the daily operations.

Some of you may wonder how I was able to reconcile my anxiety about internal corruption with my wish for redundancy from daily operations. I did so by recognizing that corruption is an inherent part of human nature and the Indian psyche. It would not matter if I was physically present or not; if people wanted to be corrupt, they would find a way. All I could do was strengthen my system of checks and balances and trust my staff.

I instituted another RoL policy within the company. The rule stated that if any employee was found screaming or shouting, they would be fined Rs 500. The idea went back to the source. The more you screamed, the lesser your RoL.

The next important lesson that I carried from Harvard was the importance of controlling overheads. I cannot stress this enough; overheads are the silent killers in any organization. It is only when you identify your overheads and figure out where you stand in the industry can you become more profitable. This brought me to an important point. I could identify my overheads.

Say, I have an overhead of Rs 100. Is that good or bad? I needed a benchmark to compare my overheads. I found the solution by starting a benchmarking exercise with 15 other garment exporters in the National Capital Region with the help of the Okhla Garment Textile Cluster (OGTC). This cluster has helped us so much in improving ourselves and I would encourage every exporter to join such clusters that foster growth and improvement.

We wanted to set the benchmarks ourselves. The first thing we did was to identify and define an overhead. What expenses could fit within that definition? Then we compared our individual overheads with each of the others. The 15 garment exporters came from Okhla, Faridabad, and Gurgaon. The cluster helped us to understand our overheads better.

We could find areas where we could improve or cut costs. We did so by comparing the number of pieces we manufactured across a set time period. Then we compared our sales across the same period. We compared using percentages without revealing any proprietary information. We were able to customize the information and data for ourselves. One of the revelations that we came across was that factories based in Delhi had greater overheads compared to the overheads of factories based in Noida, Faridabad, and Gurgaon. It was not surprising. Slowly garment exporters have been moving out of Delhi to places where the labor is cheaper and also the corresponding overheads. The reason why areas like Gurgaon, Faridabad, and Noida have become powerful manufacturing centers is because of lower wages and more industry-friendly local governments. Our time at Harvard gave us a base of security that we did not know we needed. The experiences gave us some much-needed perspective.

We learned from our professors and our diverse cast of classmates. Our perspectives were widened. I can confidently state that if I had not gone to Harvard, I would have been the stereotypical Punjabi businessman stuck to his methods. I would have looked to micromanage every operation and not focused on the growth.

Our vision has grown so broad that we have even discussed the idea of taking *Saivana* public and are working toward it. We gained such confidence due to the tremendous levels of growth *Saivana* has experienced post-Harvard. We have become a smooth and efficient company. We run with great efficiency and effectiveness. We did so by adopting a practice that flies against convention.

We used to have 29 to 30 buyers. After our time at Harvard, we decided to cut our relationships with 18 buyers. I like to describe these 18 clients as the ones who did not contribute to our top line or bottom line; they contributed to my headache line. They used to constantly doubt us and harangue us with daily phone calls and long email chains.

After we processed their existing orders, we bid them farewell. People were shocked and could not comprehend our decision. I explained that we had limited resources and we needed to focus on our core customers. We were far removed from the days of rolling suitcases full of clothes across cities trying to land clients. We identified nine clients. We identified them on the basis of trust and the potential they held in carving their own niche in the market.

We knew that these nine clients would make a mark in the market, and we wanted in on the ride. The final lesson I learned from Harvard was the importance of suppliers.

There are many adages and phrases that say that you need to treat your employees as assets. Harvard taught us the need to recognize suppliers as a part of our core system. Thus, they also need to be looked at through the prism of being assets. I can say with pride that *Saivana*, in its history, has never missed a single salary payment or a supplier payment. Of course, there have been disputes with suppliers when they supplied shoddy materials. However, we have never failed our obligations.

As I mentioned in one of the earlier chapters, our suppliers never had to wait more than 20 minutes in our office to receive their checks. The times have has changed, and we now do a direct bank transfer. We know that their time is as equally precious as ours. It is because of our commitment and treatment of our suppliers that many businesses across Indian want to become part of *Saivana*'s suppliers.

Extra Customization:

- The biggest contributor to the Rs 500 per scream fund was me, Rajat Sikka. I needed time to get myself in balance. There are moments when I do lose my temper. But I find that those occasions have become fewer over the years.

- On a related note, the greatest overhead contribution to *Saivana* also came from one singular source, Rajat Sikka. I knew that I had to separate myself from *Saivana*. *Saivana* was an entity of its own. Check your overheads; you may be surprised like me to find yourself as the biggest contributor.

- OGTC is a robust organization these days and even has a website: www.ogtc.in

- One of the major ways you can develop the youth and have them stay long-term in your company is to ensure that your company is dedicated to growth. Do not become comfortable. Once you allow the company to stagnate, the people within will also want to stagnate. After Harvard, I have the lowest rates of employee attrition in *Saivana*'s history.
  Remember that people want to associate themselves with great companies. You can only do that if you are committed to growth. When your employees are asked where they work, they should be able to answer with pride.

On more than one occasion, my employees have told me of how people were impressed with them when they answered *Saivana*. More than a few of their questioners even asked if they could help them land a job in *Saivana*.

8
THE CRÈME DE LA CRÈME

"Your time is limited, so don't waste it living someone else's life. Don't be trapped by dogma – which is living with the results of other people's thinking. Don't let the noise of other's opinions drown out your own inner voice. And most important, have the courage to follow your heart and intuition. They somehow already know what you truly want to become. Everything else is secondary." – Steve Jobs

If you are a budding entrepreneur, here are a few important points to remember. The cream always rises to the top. There are countless businesses that have failed to take off. I have gleaned the following learnings from my experience with *Saivana*.

1. Do not lose patience.

One of the greatest virtues that you will need if you want to be an entrepreneur is patience. There will be countless times when you will feel like you are failing. It is vital that you persevere through the lean times. There will be occasions, especially in the initial three to four years, when the world will offer you better chances. Do not lose patience at any cost.

You will be tempted into taking a job as the business does not seemingly take off. There will be familial and societal pressures as well. People around you will try to convince you that a job would guarantee a secure and reliable source of income. This will be especially true if you are newly married or a new parent. Do not lose the conviction of your purpose. There is nothing wrong with having second thoughts. However, get over them quickly. There were more than a few occasions where I second-guessed myself. In the first few years of *Saivana*, I used to check for jobs in the Middle East. As mentioned earlier, I was educated abroad, and I felt the distinct pangs of inadequacy when I was stuck in the back roads of Tughlaqabad. I could see myself in a well-paying job that would help my young family instead of cutting threads in what was essentially a sweatshop. However, I was able to hold on, and thus *Saivana* has become a success today.

2. Do not lose passion.

One of the chief reasons why businesses fail is the lack of passion or a decrease in passion among entrepreneurs. If you are truly passionate about your business, you will find that you will have an inexhaustible amount of patience. You will be plagued by second thoughts when you are not truly passionate about your business. The passion for *Saivana* came from Vandana. I could see that she had a natural talent and flair for fashion. I, on the other hand, was not exactly versed in the field. I was used to being a part of the daily grind of office life. Before jumping into *Saivana*, I had hated the nine-to-five grind.

I used to look forward to the time I could log out. No job is worth it if you are ruled by the temptation to look at the clock at regular intervals to determine the clocking-out time.

However, I was driven by my resentment of the office grind into business. I was lucky that Vandana was extremely talented and passionate about fashion. I took my cues from her. My job, as I saw it, was to protect and nurture her talent.

I saw it as my personal responsibility to ensure that she only had to worry about the fashion part. I built the other necessary systems around her, such as the marketing, finance, and sales departments. I wanted to shield her from the troubles of inspections and labor disputes. I can say with confidence that without Vandana, *Saivana* would have ceased to exist.

Stick to your core competency when you are in business. You may see an opportunity to branch out to other areas. But when you branch out, you will lose your passion. So, stick to your core competency. If you are good at and passionate about manufacturing, do not venture out into HR consulting.

3.   Hire the right people.

For an entrepreneur, there is no greater step that needs the correct choice than the hiring of the right people. Just think about the time people take to hire domestic help for their homes. If you need to hire a cook, you will ensure to find out if the person is reliable and good. You will ask for reviews from friends and neighbors. You would not want to compromise on the quality of your life. Likewise, it is important that you hire the right people. You need to approach hiring labor and retaining employees with the correct mindset. Many entrepreneurs in India view employees in the wrong light. I have come across many entrepreneurs at parties and gatherings who deem the seventh day of every month as a burdensome day. Why do they think so? Because they have to pay salaries to their staff.

I have never understood this view. These employees are the ones who create value for the company. Then why are they viewed from such a negative angle? If you were to look at the balance sheet of any company, the employees are seen as liabilities. They are considered so as they have to be paid salaries. However, do not look at your employees as payables. Look at them as receivables. Look at how you receive value from their work. My greatest joy in *Saivana* is seeing how my employees are able to create value in their own lives.

Some of them are able to send their kids to the best colleges. Some have been able to build a new house. Do not resent such successes. Take pride in their achievements.

When you treat your employees with such respect, they will rise to the challenge of taking your enterprise to greater heights. Finding the right people is never easy. There is no magic solution. It is a process of trial and error. Many people will talk a big game in their interviews or blatantly lie on their resumes. You will be able to spot them when they start working in your company. You must identify the ones who are faking it immediately. My one piece of advice to you—be cold-hearted. Let them go. If your gut feeling says that someone is not suited to your company, heed that instinct. Just think of the rot it can cause if you allow such elements to continue working in your company.

Other honest employees will see the signal that inefficient and toxic colleagues are allowed to stay and will be left despondent. I saw this from *Saivana's* ventures in America. We tried to set up an American subsidiary in 2008. We tried for four years, and then we had to shut it down.

There were a few people who should not have been allowed to stay and consequently, the team failed to create any value leading to the shutdown of the American arm of *Saivana*. At *Saivana* today, I ensure to remind my staff that their salaries are paid by the buyers and not me. *Saivana* is just the intermediary. If their work is shoddy, the buyer will refuse to pay. It would mean that the staff at *Saivana* would not be paid, and some of them may even have to be let go. I do so to remind them of the quality of work expected of them. Hire people who have failed in life. The road to success is paved with failure. As I explained earlier, you are not looking to hire the perfect candidate. You are looking to hire the candidate with the perfect response to failure. Pay your staff on time. I can say with great pride that *Saivana* is a well-known organization with a great reputation worldwide. One of the key factors behind it is the satisfaction of our employees and suppliers.

4. Keep your suppliers happy.

Treat your suppliers well. How you treat your suppliers will be reciprocated by your buyer. *Saivana* has never missed a payment to a supplier. There have been a couple of occasions when the accounts department has told me that they had not received a call intimating payment. I have never been taken in by that remark. If the due date for the payment has been agreed on in advance, make the payment. Why should you wait for the supplier to intimate you?

5. Be wary of customer demands.

Be wary of your buyers. In the previous chapter, I talked about how some companies contributed to my headache line. Be wary of such buyers. One of the greatest lessons you need to learn is that you should never overcommit. I have seen many Indian exporters use the phrase, 'No problem.' If you say no problem, inevitably, there will be a problem.

Learn to say no. I have seen many exporters agreeing to take on a new buyer when they do not have the capacity to commit. They do so because they want more clients. What do you think will happen six months down the line? You will be either delayed in your deliveries or will end up shipping goods of substandard quality. When that happens, your clients will be disgruntled with you. It could lead to resentment, and they could spread your infamy.

Always remember that when you overcommit, you are only jeopardizing your company. You only need to look at some of the biggest failures in recent times like Theranos, WeWork, and Fyre Festival. All of them came with glitzy adverts and promises. However, when it was time to deliver, they failed spectacularly. I want you to remember that reputations are not built on Instagram stories or social media likes. Reputations are built on the quality of your work and word of mouth. If your clients are disgruntled with your work, they will talk to other potential clients, and they will all avoid you. You also need to be wary of your buyers.

Do not blindly accept orders. Look for quality rather than quantity. There is nothing wrong with being choosy when it comes to your buyers. Bad buyers will derail your business.

6. RoI versus RoL

Ensure to keep your focus on RoL. It is inevitable that in the first four to five years of your company, the RoL will be at rock bottom. You have to negotiate many challenges. You will have to deal with being a start-up. You have to contend with other bigger fish to carve your niche in the market. You may have to deal with the harassment of the inspectors.

However, once you are semi-successful, ensure to pay attention to your RoL. You only have one life. Learn to take time and enjoy it. Do not be plagued by bitterness. There will be occasions when you feel resentful toward others. Maybe the resentment is deserved. There is nothing wrong with feeling those emotions. But do not allow them to rule your life.

7. Focus on your overheads.

The greatest boon you can provide your business is to reduce your overheads. Do not lose sight of how much you contribute toward it personally. I remember coming across this case study at Harvard. Pepsi and Coca-Cola source their cans from other companies. Why do such massive companies not have their own canning plants? The answer is simple. The canning industry has one of the narrowest margins. It can be a challenging market and very tough to enter. Cans are sold to these companies at 15 to 20 cents.

There is not much scope for profit. Then there is the company, Crown Holdings, formerly known as Crown Cork and Seal. It is one of the leading companies in canning and is a billion-dollar company. They managed to close out 96 straight quarters with new heights achieved. How did they do it? Their CEO managed to bring down the overheads from 28 percent to 6 percent.

His office was sparse and spartan in its décor, and he would only choose red-eye flights to travel as they were the cheapest.

8. Make yourself redundant from the company operations.

As an entrepreneur, you need to separate yourself from the daily operations. One of the best examples is that of Schlumberger. It is one of the leading oil rigging companies in the world and is a multi-billion-dollar company. The CEO of the company was once found filing nails in his office.

People were bewildered by his behavior. When asked if he did not have any work, he answered that he did not as he had hired the best staff around him. They looked to solve the problems. He only had to step in if they were unable to solve them. However, as he had hired the best staff, they were able to solve the problems themselves. He focused on the growth and strategy of the company and not fighting fires in daily operations. Learn to separate yourself from the business. I have already mentioned how *Saivana* revolved around Vandana. Can the company exist without Vandana? Today, I am proud to say that the answer is yes. However, she remains as the mentor within the company as the buyers still trust her.

9. Do not live in a toxic household

I can say with experience, living in a toxic household will only damage you and your business. If you are constantly facing pressures and doubts from your family, it can be toxic. Entrepreneurship, especially in the manufacturing sector, is not for the faint-hearted. If you are planning to start a manufacturing business, you will find me more discouraging as it is one of the toughest sectors to make your mark.

There are so many regulatory challenges, and it can be a bruising experience. The new value creators are found in the tech sector, be it finance or blockchain technology.

You can create more value in those areas. When I mentor many people, I always look to dissuade them from entering manufacturing as it can be extremely troublesome. The consequences are that you will get into disagreements with your family members and other members of your social circle. All these disagreements will lead to fights. They are inevitable. If you find yourself in a toxic environment, look to remove yourself from it.

One of the biggest losses that Vandana and I have suffered is that we missed out on our daughters' childhood. We focused too much on *Saivana* during their formative years. While we have cut back and made time for the family now, it remains our greatest regret. Our lives have turned for the better as we are now more focused on sustenance and quality of life. Another personal regret of mine is the number of court cases I have had to deal with involving my loved ones. I have been estranged from my relatives.

However, it has been the consequence of my father not having a succession plan in place. It is one lesson that I intend on never forgetting. I will never leave my daughters a legacy of debt and legal cases. Indians have always looked at will-writing with suspicion. They look at it as plot points of stories in the West. However, ensure that you have your will written and notarized. It should detail your succession plan so that your children are not stuck in courts fighting for their share.

Speaking of legal cases, do not get embroiled in legal cases. Always look to avoid them. Look to settle cases out of court quickly. I am reminded of a story here. Once upon a time, there was a village full of Shaivites and Vaishnavites. As the names indicated, half of the village prayed to Lord Vishnu, and the other half prayed to Lord Shiva. One day, they came across an injured elephant. The whole village nurtured it back to health. The elephant was moved by their kindness and did not leave the village. The villagers were elated when they found this out. They could now have an elephant in their temple. There could be no greater sign of auspiciousness. However, there was a problem: the village had two temples with the devotees following two distinct faiths. To whom would the elephant belong?

Both the factions got into an altercation and when they realized that neither side had any intention of backing down, they went to court. They argued and countersued for years. Finally, a decision was taken in the highest land of the court, and the winning party jubilantly rushed home to their village. Alas! When they reached the village, they learned that the elephant had passed away the previous night. It is a part and parcel of the Indian judicial system. Legal cases can take years to resolve. The only winners in a prolonged legal dispute are the lawyers.

10. Some things come with the territory.

Corruption is like cancer that can eat away at a company. It is inevitable. Build a strong and robust system with enough points for checks and balances. When you have a system that is robust, you will be able to spot corruption quickly. I also have the two theories that I mentioned previously. Be wary of people who never take a day off. Be wary of people who are getting fat around their bellies. It is more than likely that they are eating into the company's profits. The reality for small and medium-sized enterprises is that 'inspector raaj' exists and has to be dealt with. Make your peace and live with it. Do not lose your cool with the inspectors. Play nice so that you are not stuck paying fines.

ABOUT THE AUTHOR

Rajat Sikka is the Managing Director and co-founder of one of the premier fashion houses in Saivana Exports, New Delhi. Saivana is among the top Indian sustainable garment exporter in high fashion ladies' and children's garments. Rajat set up Saivana in 1994 and works with some of the leading fashion designers across the globe today.

Rajat Sikka is a marketing expert and has excellent man-management skills. Having experienced the struggles of entrepreneurship, Rajat is a source of advice and guidance to many budding entrepreneurs today. He is an avid angel investor in numerous startups and loves mentoring young people to achieve their dreams. Rajat can be found on the golf course trying to perfect his game in his spare time.

#

Lightning Source UK Ltd.
Milton Keynes UK
UKHW040046170522
403106UK00004B/80